TCCB

The Test and County Cricket Board Collection

CRICKET

◄ HEROES ►

TCCB

The Test and County Cricket Board Collection

CRICKET

◄ HEROES ►

ESSAYS ON ENGLAND'S FINEST PLAYERS
BY ENGLAND'S FINEST WRITERS

Edited by Peter Hayter

BLOOMSBURY

Sports Editions Limited

Managing Director	Richard Dewing
Art Director	Mary Hamlyn
Senior Designer	Rob Kelland
Designers	Sandra Cowell
	Adrian Waddington
Editor	Leslie Smillie
Picture Research	Sandra Cowell
	Abigail Sims

First published in 1990 by
Bloomsbury Publishing Limited
2 Soho Square
London
W1V 5DE

ISBN 0-7475-0508-X

Produced, edited and designed by
Sports Editions Limited
3 Greenlea Park
Prince George's Road
London
SW19 2JD

Typeset in Bodoni and 20th Century by Sports Editions Limited

Origination, printing and binding by Butler and Tanner, Frome

Cover illustrations of Boycott, Dexter, Gower, Compton, Trueman, Botham and Grace by Gavin Harrison

c r i c k e t h e r o e s

PREFACE

There are two ways, it seems to me, to go about the business of books. First, there is the hard way, writing them yourself. Then there is the easy way, having other people write them for you. In this respect, my involvement in this book represents a triumph for the easy way.

Cricket Heroes belongs not to me, but to the writers and, more importantly, to the cricketers who made it worth writing. Cricket, more than any other sport, thrives on the written word. Through the years, men such as C. L. R. James, Neville Cardus, Jack Fingleton and R. C. Robertson-Glasgow built reputations not as cricket writers but as writers who wrote about cricket. They set the standard by which all others are judged. What typified their work was the implicit understanding that the game is an avenue of expression for the human character. I hope that what you read of the work of those who have followed indicates that the same rules still apply.

I would like to thank the writers; Tim Crow of the Test and County Cricket Board for his enthusiasm and invaluable assistance; Geoffrey Copinger for providing the statistics for each player; Leslie Smillie and Matthew Hamlyn; Sandra Cowell for her diligent picture research; all the photographers whose work illuminates the book; and Mary Hamlyn and her team of designers.

Finally, I would like to thank my father, Reg Hayter, for helping me to appreciate cricket and cricket writing.

Peter Hayter
St Kitts
February 1990

CONTENTS

c r i c k e t   h e r o e s

CONTENTS

c r i c k e t   h e r o e s

LES AMES

Tony Pawson

Leslie Ethelbert George Ames was a Kentish legend in the great Kentish tradition of wicket-keeper batsmen of Test class. With Huish and Hubble as fine exemplars for him to follow, Ames developed his own inimitable style just as Godfrey Evans and Alan Knott were later to develop theirs. As a wicket-keeper Ames adopted the Quaker philosophy of studying to be quiet and impeccably correct. No raucous Duckworth-type appeals from him, nor any of Evans's flamboyance, nor of Knott's acrobatic agility. One bail removed and a polite enquiry of the umpire was the Ames approach.

One bail removed was a hallmark also of a different era of cricket in which great spinners flourished and the wicket-keeping job was inevitably more demanding and more important. The most remarkable of all such combinations was that of 'Tich' Freeman and Les Ames. When Freeman took an incredible 304 wickets in a season in 1928, the 300th victim was Richard Tyldesley, appropriately stumped by Ames. Of Ames's 842 victims while playing for Kent, 512 were caught and 330 stumped. The modern difference is well expressed by only 87 of Alan Knott's total of 915 being stumped.

The MCC Coaching Book laid it down as an unarguable principle that the best wicket-keeper must always be chosen regardless of batting ability. That was sensible enough in Ames's day, but is outdated in the present game. The emphasis on speed and the virtual elimination of true wrist spin means that English 'keepers stand back most of the time and the vast majority of chances are easy by comparison with standing up to spinners. So it became sensible to include the likes of Jim Parks in a Test team when his batting so improved the balance of the side that it outweighed the fact that he was not in the top six 'keepers in the country. Alan Knott's superior batting also ensured his place as of right, making him first choice for many years despite the matching talent of Bob Taylor as a world-class 'keeper.

Happily no such decision ever had to be made about Ames since the selectors could confidently pick him as the best 'keeper and as also worth his place as a batsman. 2,434 runs in 47 Tests for an impressive average of 40.56 was proof enough of that, as was the tally of 74 caught and 23 stumped of his main skill. There was an added value to his batting in the textbook purity of his stroke

c r i c k e t   h e r o e s

LES AMES

play, the attraction of his powerful straight driving and the speed of his scoring. Three of the best examples of that are Ames's swift 202 not out in Kent's record total of 803 for 4 made in seven hours against Essex at Brentwood in 1934, coming in after Ashdown and Woolley had put on 352 in the highest ever partnership for Kent — a massacre of tired bowling. Gloucestershire's attack was fresh enough when Ames hit 70 in just 36 minutes as Kent scored 219 for 2 in 71 minutes to race to a win at Dover in August 1937. The different attitude of those days is clear from Tom Goddard's analysis of 8.2 overs for 98 runs. Who today would allow a slow bowler to continue like that when opponents have a race against the clock? In Tests there was his remarkable partnership with 'Gubby' Allen against New Zealand in 1931 as 246 runs in under three hours transformed the score from 190 for 7, with Ames making 137.

Les Ames behind the stumps for Kent against Sussex in 1932. He made a remarkable total of 441 stumpings in his career.

Les had been educated at the Harvey Grammar School in Folkestone and it was at Folkestone that he made 295 against Gloucestershire, his highest score. That was in 1933, his best batting season, when he totalled 3,058 runs. When I started to play for Kent after the war either Evans or Levett kept wicket while Ames was our premier batsman and occasional bowler of crafty legbreaks. Oh yes, Les could bowl as well, with 24 wickets at an average of 33.37. The most amusing of these was seeing him beat and bowl Mike Ainsworth on 99 — Mike certainly didn't think it funny as he had been promised a special present if he made a century.

Cricket statistics can be worse than damned lies if they take no regard of conditions or opposition strength. Yet just as Bradman's extraordinary Test average makes it a waste of time to indulge in any argument about who is the best batsman of all time so Les's run totals, batting first wicket down for Kent, indicate just how good he was then. In both 1947 and 1949 he topped two thousand runs despite being in his forties and plagued by occasional back trouble. That trouble had cost him a season's cricket in 1936 and was to bring

LES AMES

an abrupt termination to his playing career in 1951. His overall record would be even more remarkable but for the years lost to the war and a bad back.

My happiest memory of batting with him was in a partnership at Canterbury which set up a win over Middlesex with seven minutes to spare and also brought him his hundredth hundred to spark a delighted cacophony from the hooting horns and the cheering crowd. His straight driving was a wonder to behold that day as three men on the boundary behind the bowler hardly touched the ball as it flew over or between them, so powerful was his hitting, so accurate his placing. His 131 in two hours won the match with my own 57 contributing to a partnership of 85 in 37 minutes.

Les was born at Elham on 3rd December 1905 and as a youngster was soon absorbing the unique atmosphere of the Canterbury weeks of those days with the tents, the bands, and the added colour of Ladies Day. My father, himself a first-class wicket-keeper who was four years in the Oxford side, claimed that he spotted Les's potential in a club game and told the County. The truth is that the potential was so obvious anyone could spot it and in 1926 Les played his first two matches for the County, taking four catches in one of them — in the outfield.

Next year he had his first relatively full season, beginning to take over from Hubble as 'keeper and scoring more than a thousand runs. With G. B. Legge succeeding A. J. Evans as captain, Kent finished as runners-up in 1928 largely due to the partnership of Ames and Freeman. That was the year 'Tich' took 304 wickets, 246 of them for Kent, while Ames in all caught 69 and stumped 52, a record. Next year Ames went six better in victims, his brilliance soon being accorded the recognition which was to bring him 47 Test caps.

In 1928 he played for an England XI against a West Indies team defeated already in the Tests. His score of 42 was the highest in the first innings, with Woolley winning the match with an inspired second innings 151. His Kent colleagues Woolley and Freeman were also primarily responsible for winning the third and fourth Tests against South Africa the following year which allowed the selectors to displace Duckworth at last — and give Ames his chance (Ames had been on the winter tour to Australia, but was not picked for any Test). Les was out for a duck, but his keeping was as cool and impeccable as ever.

c r i c k e t   h e r o e s

LES AMES

By the time of the famous (or infamous according to your viewpoint) 'bodyline' series the roles were reversed with Duckworth the permanent reserve. Les did score 69 at Adelaide, but otherwise it was his keeping, rather than his batting, which produced impressive results. Not so in 1934 against Australia. He and Leyland just failed to save the first Test with a courageous 70 minute stand against Bill O'Reilly, who was almost unplayable on a crumbling pitch. Ames's 120 in the next Test contributed to squaring the series, with Australia beaten by an innings as Verity took 15 wickets on a rain-damaged pitch. Ames caught Bradman off a skier with the great man never at his best on a difficult wicket, and out to a wild slog just as the pitch was easing.

The fifth Test was the decider and so a timeless one. That suited Bradman and Ponsford, who launched Australia to victory with individual scores of 244 and 266. In the England reply Ames himself was well set on 33 when he ricked his back and had to retire. This gave Kent another wicket-keeping record, albeit unwelcome. Frank Woolley took over behind the stumps and let a record number of byes to add to the misery of a final Test in which he scored 4 and 0.

Ames's contribution to cricket was far from being confined to his playing days. These ended sadly at the very start of the 1951 season. In the first match against Nottinghamshire at Gillingham Ames was in pain after ricking his back again when fielding. He had not meant to bat, but six wickets fell quickly. Courageous and committed as always Les struggled to the wicket. In his own words he then "went to play a ball round to leg and just collapsed in a heap. It was my last game."

So there was no nostalgic farewell match and the tributes were reserved for later. A special feature article in the County's annual read: "It was not only what Les Ames did, but the way he did it, which will mark him for all time as one of the finest exponents of the game of cricket. His whole-hearted enthusiasm and extraordinary efficiency were only equalled by his personal modesty. He might have earned his place in any team by his wicket-keeping or his batting alone, but he had not the single-mindedness of the specialist. Always a great-hearted player, his best efforts were at the disposal of the captain as long as the game was in progress."

Those achievements were recognised by his being elected an Honorary Life Member of the MCC — a rare distinction for a professional, and a Life-Member

c r i c k e t   h e r o e s

LES AMES

of Kent. That county he continued to serve, being Manager in 1957 and later a very shrewd Secretary/Manager, helping Kent to a period of success. Appropriately he went out this time on a high note, retiring in 1974 after Kent won the Gillette Cup. The Kent connection continued, though, through the Hoppers Tie Club, of which he remained controller until his death in February of this year. This was inaugurated by Les, Bryan Valentine and 'Hopper' Levett when the County produced a tie which the players were not allowed to wear.

One of the shrewdest England captains under whom Les played was Bob Wyatt. His view of Ames was unequivocal: "The best batsman/wicket-keeper England has ever possessed. Makes few mistakes behind the wicket and is particularly quick when stumping. He is a forceful batsman who is very quick on his feet and a good player of slow bowling. Drives well and is a fine exponent of the on-drive. He is also a fine slip and very quick in the outfield."

In cricket terms and as a man Ames was indeed a Jack of all trades, and Master of all.

L. E. G. AMES KENT
BORN 3.12.05, ELHAM, KENT

BATTING

	Matches	Innings	Not out	Runs	High score	Avg	100
Test	47	72	12	2,434	149	40.56	8
First class	593	951	95	37,248	295	43.51	102

BOWLING AND FIELDING

	Runs	Wickets	Avg	5 W/I	10 W/M	BB	Ct	St
Test	0	0	0	0	0	0	74	23
First class	801	24	33.37	0	0	3/23	703	418

TREVOR BAILEY

John Woodcock

In the 1950s Trevor Bailey became a symbol of resistance. When England were in trouble on the cricket field, people would say: "It'll be all right, Bailey's still there." It was a reputation based more on intense application than great natural ability, and it had its origins at Lord's on June 30th 1953, when, with Willie Watson of Yorkshire, he shared in one of the greatest of all match-saving partnerships.

It has to be remembered that those were the days when a Test Match between England and Australia had the whole country by the ears — much as happens in Australia now for the running of the Melbourne Cup. The market had yet to be flooded with one-day internationals. In 1953 it was 15 years and a World War since England had beaten Australia, and longer than that since they had held the Ashes. Another defeat seemed imminent when, with England 73 for four in their second innings and still 269 runs adrift, Bailey joined Watson 50 minutes before lunch on the last day at Lord's. When the next wicket fell it was nearly six o'clock and England were safe.

Trevor Bailey in 1953, the year in which he featured in a match-saving partnership with Willie Watson for England.

Next morning the *Manchester Guardian* led its front page with Neville Cardus's report, headlined 'Miracle of Faith at Lord's.' Someone else came up with 'Barnacle Bailey.' When, later in the same series, Bailey denied Australia for a second time — by batting 4 hours and 20 minutes for 38 and then using every device to hold them up with the ball — he became a marked man. The last ditch was his spiritual home, and no-one was to come to know it better than the Australians.

The forward defensive stroke was Trevor's trademark, the bat well out in front of the pad rather than wedged against it as it would be today. As a bowler, he gave thought to every ball. Close to the wicket he held some brilliant catches. In his first-class career he scored 28,641 runs, took 2,082 wickets, caught 428 batsmen and stonewalled countless thousands of spectators into a state of stupor. In 215 of his 1,072 innings he finished not out, and if, in doing so, he had saved a seemingly lost cause, he went to bed a happy man.

Born at Westcliff-on-Sea on December 3rd, 1923, Bailey was fortunate to be coached at his preparatory school by Denys Wilcox, who had captained Cambridge and Essex, and then at Dulwich College by C. S. Marriott, who had

TREVOR BAILEY

bowled leg breaks for Kent and once for England. Bailey had five years in the Dulwich side, combining with A. W. H. Mallett in 1941 and 1942 to make them more than a match for the schools they played. While in the Royal Marines from 1943 until 1946 the name he had made for himself at school meant that he was on the mailing list for war-time matches at Lord's when stationed within reach. He was in the Cambridge sides of 1947 and 1948, and played the first of his 61 Test Matches, against New Zealand, in 1949. Once in the England side he stayed there without a break, other than for the occasional injury or when MCC went to India or Pakistan, until the end of the tour to Australia in 1958-59.

His career with Essex ran from 1946 until 1967. At different times he was assistant secretary, secretary and captain. If he was not in his office, which was a caravan for much of the summer, he was usually to be found batting or bowling. He and Doug Insole, who had first played together at Cambridge, were at that time the style and substance of Essex cricket — they gave it its stability and character — but despite their best efforts the county championship eluded them.

Bailey did the double of 1,000 runs and 100 wickets eight times. Since 1937 he stands alone in having scored 2,000 runs and taken 100 wickets in a season (1959). He is one of only four Englishmen to have scored more than 2,000 runs and taken over 100 wickets in Test cricket. He was what all successful Test sides need, unless they have a pack of very fast bowlers, namely a genuine all-rounder. Of the five series he played in against Australia, England won three.

Another ovation for Bailey, this time following a crucial 38 scored in 260 minutes to save England from defeat.

Having opened the bowling in his first Test Match, at Headingley, he opened the batting in his last, at Melbourne. When, at Melbourne, Ray Lindwall yorked him in the second innings, it meant a 'pair' for Bailey but took the great Lindwall past Clarrie Grimmett's previous Australian record of 215 Test wickets. Lindwall paid Bailey the compliment of saying that the record felt all the better for having fallen as it did. For Bailey aroused in his opponents a powerful, if sometimes grudging, respect. I am sure West Indians of his own generation would agree with that. Having bowled them out by the evening of the first day of the last Test Match at Kingston, Jamaica, in 1953-54, he then added insult to injury by going in first with his captain, Len Hutton, and still

TREVOR BAILEY

being there at close of play 35 minutes later. Less helpfully, his 68 in seven hours and 38 minutes against Australia at Brisbane in 1958-59 did a good deal more for Australia's morale than England's.

To younger generations it must seem strange that with his sharp eye for the game he was never seriously canvassed for the England captaincy. If he were playing today, he certainly would be. As it is, he commentates knowingly and nasally, but never noisily, for the BBC, moves genially around the cricket scene, and simply hates to see an England side failing for want of a disciplined approach. He would have been a fiendishly effective one-day bowler, and no bad one-day batsman. At Brisbane in 1954-55, when an Australian philanthropist offered £100 to the first Englishman to hit a six, Bailey very soon won the money. He was, you understand, nothing if not deliberate.

In the nets at Chingford, Essex getting in some batting practice.

T. E. BAILEY ESSEX
BORN 3.12.23, WESTCLIFF-ON-SEA, ESSEX

BATTING

	Matches	Innings	Not out	Runs	High score	Avg	100
Test	61	91	14	2,290	134*	29.74	1
First class	682	1,072	215	28,641	205	33.42	28

BOWLING AND FIELDING

	Runs	Wickets	Avg	5 W/I	10 W/M	BB	Ct	St
Test	3,856	132	29.21	5	1	7/34	32	0
First class	48,170	2,082	23.13	110	13	10/90	428	0

cricket heroes

SYDNEY BARNES

ooooooooooooooooooooooooooooooooooooooooooooooooooooooooooooooooooooooooooooooooooooooooooooooooooo

Brian Bearshaw

No man has gone into English cricket history with such a high reputation from so little county and Test experience as Sydney Barnes. He played 46 times for Lancashire, four for Warwickshire and 27 for England in a first-class career which extended over 37 seasons and which brought him 719 wickets at 17.09 each in 133 games. But it should be remembered that he played without the daily grind of county cricket which can so easily bring on staleness. Perhaps Barnes, like many Test cricketers, would have had to ration his energies if he had played 400 times for Lancashire instead of 46, as well as playing for England, and maybe his record would not have been the formidable one it is. He found the daily demands of county cricket too irksome, and settled, instead, for the gentler requirements of league and Minor Counties cricket where he could take wickets by the sackful without breaking into a sweat.

Barnes was born in Smethwick in Staffordshire on April 19, 1873, and did not take up cricket seriously until he joined his town team at the age of 18. He received little coaching but soon learned to bowl off breaks and leg breaks at a fast-medium pace. He had a perfect action, a springy run-up with his arm straight and as high as possible at the point of delivery. He had an impeccable length and a line which made batsmen play every ball. And he spun the ball sharply. Don Bradman once argued that Bill O'Reilly had claims to a higher position than Barnes among history's great bowlers. "O'Reilly had all the tricks of Barnes, plus one which Barnes hadn't — the googly," said Bradman. Neville Cardus told Barnes about Bradman's opinion. "He's quite right," said Barnes, "I didn't bowl the googly. I never needed it."

Barnes played a little for Warwickshire before becoming a professional in the Lancashire League where he found the games played in a different spirit to that he had been accustomed to in the Birmingham League. He was not used to that extra keenness to win, a keenness that got into his system because he felt everything depended on him. It was this spirit, he thought, which made him a fighter and a perfectionist. And which made him so unpopular, even among his fellow players. He himself later admitted: "I was a difficult man to play with. I did my best at all times and expected the others to do the same." And when they did not, he fumed and raged.

c r i c k e t   h e r o e s

ALEC BEDSER

probable movement in the air and off the pitch, were the few, very few, deliveries one could leave alone. I cannot recall a full toss, and half volleys were as rare as a truthful politician.

After that disastrous experiment of relying upon an all-seam attack in Brisbane, Alec was dropped for the second Test, which England won, and a typhoon called Tyson began to blow Australian batsmen away. It sadly signalled the end of his distinguished international career in which he took 236 wickets in 51 Tests. Ironically the conditions in Sydney were tailor-made for the 'Big Fella', as it was one of the few occasions when I relied on swing rather than movement off the seam, and I am convinced he would have captured at least six wickets in the first innings and therefore remained in the side for at least the next two Tests.

An example of the flowing Bedser style.

Alec continued to play for Surrey, for whom he took 1,459 wickets at 19 apiece, until 1960, but that was not to be the end of his long association with international and county cricket, which meant so much to him. He went on to become England's longest-serving selector, was Chairman from 1969 to 1981, managed England on several overseas tours, and was President of Surrey. A sound and sensible selector (unpaid, of course), Alec did experience some difficulty in coming to terms with standards which were different from those he had been brought up on, while at times he was a little short of imagination. He must wonder these days at the considerable sums of money now being paid to a number of individuals for doing the job which he did for nothing, for so long, and far more successfully.

A. V. BEDSER   SURREY
BORN 4.7.18, READING, BERKSHIRE

BATTING

	Matches	Innings	Not out	Runs	High score	Avg	100
Test	51	71	15	714	79	12.75	0
First class	485	576	181	5,735	126	14.51	1

BOWLING AND FIELDING

	Runs	Wickets	Avg	5 W/I	10 W/M	BB	Ct	St
Test	5,876	236	24.89	15	5	7/44	26	0
First class	39,279	1,924	20.41	96	16	8/18	289	0

c r i c k e t   h e r o e s

IAN BOTHAM

Alan Lee

Very few sportsmen have been the subject of *This is Your Life* at the age of 25. But then very few sportsmen bear comparison with Ian Botham. He would have been a titan purely on the strength of his cricketing deeds, but his lifestyle and personality have promoted him to the foreground of the nation's celebrities. Like so many of this elite breed, he may not universally be loved but he can never be ignored.

A young Ian Botham reels after being hit by a ball from Andy Roberts during a Benson and Hedges cup tie in 1974. After spitting out two teeth, he recovered to play a match-winning innings for Somerset.

The first thing a person learns, on coming into close contact with Ian Terence Botham, is that he is a relentless competitor. He is not happy unless he has a challenge in sight, however trivial or diverse. The second thing a person learns is that Botham expects to win. It is this indomitable optimism which has marked every phase of his cricketing life, from the time he boldly announced to England's Centenary Test side in 1977 that he would soon be taking one of their places (he did) to the time, 11 years on, when he poured scorn on those who believed that a serious back injury would finish him (it did not).

Between times, he has broken more records than I would care to recount. He has won matches which seemed irretrievably lost and he has learned to fly a plane, play baseball, drive racing cars and own racehorses. He can resemble the old-style country gentleman with his pursuits of fishing and shooting, he can hold a lucid conversation on everything from politics to medical science and he has raised many thousands of pounds for leukaemia research.

Oh yes, he has also raised hell. Quite frequently, actually. The darker, undisciplined side of his character has not always been endearing, even if some of the stories about him have been the products of either a fanciful imagination or a mischief bordering on malice. He has, and I think he would admit this much, sometimes relied on the goodwill and good nature of others to extract him from scrapes. But equally, he has never gone short of that goodwill because Botham has attracted friends of influence and importance through sheer weight of personality. On his good days, and they greatly outnumber his bad ones, he is gregarious, generous and hugely amusing. If he has sometimes surrounded himself with characters who do him little credit, this is the habitual penance of the champion sportsman, and, to date, he has always kept them under control rather than, as in some sad cases, vice-versa.

cricket heroes

IAN BOTHAM

He would probably tell you, if you were to quiz him about his greatest sporting memory, that it was not Headingley 1981 nor Bombay 1980 but a football match he played for Scunthorpe United at Bournemouth around the same time. This sums him up, for he has never been content to luxuriate in the plaudits for his cricketing heroics. Instead he has constantly sought new horizons. Had he set out to make a career in professional football he would doubtless have made a success of it, but the loss to cricket would have been incalculable.

Back in the Worcester attack after many had written him off — always a foolish thing to do — after a serious back injury.

He was born in Cheshire in 1955 but his family soon moved to Yeovil and, after a spell on the MCC groundstaff, he naturally joined Somerset in 1974. Although raw, his talent was quickly evident and the 1976 *Wisden* records: "Botham continued his development as a useful seam bowler of increasing pace, while his brilliant fielding and batting laden with potential make him a great asset." Somerset's captain at the time was Brian Close and if the rebellious young Botham was to concede respect to any elder it was to Close, a vigorous disciplinarian who believed in leading by example. Even now, when asked to nominate which cricketers he learned from, Close is the first name mentioned by Botham.

He came into the England side against the raggle-taggle 1977 Australians, a team ravaged and divided by the pickings of Kerry Packer. On his debut, Botham took five for 74 at Nottingham; in the next game at Leeds he took five for 21. England won both matches and a legend was born. England, remarkably, won 14 of the first 18 Tests in which Botham was included. At the end of that period, he had scored three centuries and taken five or more wickets in an innings no fewer than nine times

The best, though, was yet to come. In the spring of 1980 England stopped over at Bombay on their way home from Australia. They played one Test and seldom can a game at the highest level have been so utterly monopolised by one man. Botham scored 114 in his only innings and took 13 wickets. It was his

IAN BOTHAM

last match before being made England captain in succession to his guru, Mike Brearley. This, however, was not a period he remembers with any affection. He was obliged to lead two consecutive series against the formidable West Indies. England lost them both, though not disastrously, but the suspicion grew that his own irreplaceable playing talents were being impaired by responsibility. After making a 'pair' in the second Test of the 1981 series against Australia, Botham resigned, only to be told he would have been sacked anyway.

What happened next is chronicled as well as any dramatic passage in the game's history. England, one down with four to play, recalled Brearley as captain and won the next three Tests to take the Ashes. Botham's centuries, at Headingley and Old Trafford, were unforgettable; so too, his decisive bowling spell of five wickets for one run on a Sunday of high summer and even higher excitement at Edgbaston.

It is fatuous to complain that Botham has not touched such heights again. Has anyone in the annals of the game ever taken a series so firmly in hand — especially one that had begun in such personal distress ? There was, too, a good deal still in store, including the fastest-ever double-century in Test cricket, taken off the 1982 Indians and, two years on, his fifth instance of a century and five wickets in the same match. No other Test player has achieved this more than twice, a significant measure of the man's greatness.

Even in his mid-30s he hits harder and catches better than almost anyone. Written off many times, Botham refuses to go quietly. All through life, he has been the same.

On his way to a century during the remarkable Headingley Test against the Australians in 1981.

I. T. BOTHAM SOMERSET AND WORCESTERSHIRE
BORN 24.11.55, HESWALL, CHESHIRE

BATTING

	Matches	Innings	Not out	Runs	High score	Avg	100
Test	97	154	5	5,119	208	34.35	14
First class	346	533	38	16,841	228	34.02	33

BOWLING AND FIELDING

	Runs	Wickets	Avg	5 W/I	10 W/M	BB	Ct	St
Test	10,633	376	28.27	27	4	8/34	112	0
First class	28,397	1,061	26.76	56	8	8/34	317	0

c r i c k e t   h e r o e s

GEOFFREY BOYCOTT

ooooooooooooooooooooooooooooooooooooooooooooooooooooooooooooooooooooooooooooooooooooooooooooooooooo

Michael Henderson

Geoff Boycott returned to the England team after his three years of self-imposed exile and went on to score more runs for his country than any other batsman.

In the post-war years which belong to that most peculiar period, the recent past, a shy young man was growing up in the Yorkshire coalfield. He was a dedicated amateur cricketer and, though not overburdened with natural gifts, was eager to swap his clerk's job in the Ministry of Pensions for a professional career.

Early indications were not promising. Although members of his family had chipped into a kitty on his 11th birthday, to provide coaching at an indoor nets, recognition came slowly. The Yorkshire School was then the hardest. An adolescent's aptitude for hard work, by itself, impressed no-one. As he approached manhood, others, less keen, won better notices. It hurt. He gave up the clerk's job in order to practise, practise, practise. To and fro he went, from Barnsley to Leeds, an independent soul burning with purpose.

In time coaches came to admire his single-mindedness but he was far from fulfilled. Peers continued to advance, some of them from posh schools. Philip Sharpe, one such chap, did not practise four times a day, yet he was a Yorkshire first-teamer and, in 1962, was named Young Cricketer of the Year.

The bespectacled civil servant came of age the following season. He made his first championship century against Lancashire at Bramall Lane and went on to emulate Sharpe's achievement. In 1964 he won Test selection against South Africa; the next summer ended with a century in the Gillette Cup final. Old-timers were agreed, a formidable opening batsman had arrived.

By now this singular man, who spurned ale and horseplay, had earned the respect of the Yorkshire dressing room. Brian Close was still captain, Fred Trueman was charging in from the Kirkstall Lane End. There were no duffers: Illingworth, Padgett, Taylor, Binks, Wilson, Hampshire, Nicholson, Sharpe. They were heady days! From 1966 to 1968 Yorkshire won three successive championships. Yet there was unease, if not unrest, beneath the surface. Trueman retired, Close went to Somerset and Illingworth to Leicester. The gauche miner's son became, through his claim to a regular England spot, the senior pro.

He was dropped from the Test side in 1967 for slow scoring, when the selectors considered an unbeaten innings of 246 against India at Headingley to

c r i c k e t   h e r o e s

GEOFFREY BOYCOTT

The stroke which took Boycott to his century of centuries, against the Australians at Headingley in 1977.

c r i c k e t   h e r o e s

GEOFFREY BOYCOTT

be just too non troppo. But on the whole these were fruitful summers: runs, fame, acclaim.

The seasons of 1970 and 1971 were especially good. In the first year of the new decade he plundered 2,051 runs. Together with John Edrich he was one of the twin batting pillars on which Illingworth's England side contested, and won, that winter's rubber in Australia. The series set a famous year in motion. The established opener made 1,535 runs in Australia, 657 of them in five Tests. Then, returning to Yorkshire as the new county captain — still run-drunk — 2,503 more, including 13 centuries, propelled him into the record books as the first player to average more than 100 in a championship season. Eight years later, relieved of the captaincy, he was to repeat the feat.

For all his qualities, captaincy proved an elusive skill. The dedicated professional, who could count to six and judge which of two ends was safer to run to, was never equipped for collaboration. Yorkshire had good players but the team was no longer successful. Members looked covetously towards Leicester and Taunton where their exiles had put down firm roots.

"Good morning, gentlemen," a team-mate would announce each morning, pausing to add: "Good morning, Boycott." That the colleague's surname was Hutton, the public school-educated son of the man who cast the longest shadow over Yorkshire batting, must have pained him. Embattled, soon to become embittered, the captain could not bend all men to his will.

Nor would the world pay him his due. To John Arlott he was a 'lonely perfectionist', to Neville Cardus an 'honest artisan'. No moon in June romance there. "Bowling to him has always been a mixed emotion," wrote Mike Selvey, a member of the Middlesex side which won three championship titles outright and shared another under Mike Brearley. "With the elation of beating the best defence in the world goes the knowledge that in spite of his relentlessness the fielding side always has one end under control."

Frustrated by his inability to arrest Yorkshire's decline, overlooked for the England captaincy when Illingworth was chopped, the man of moods proved unable to curb his resentment. For three long years, during which English batsmen were pummelled by Lillee and Thomson in two continents, and wounded by Michael Holding at his fastest, the Test side was deprived of its straightest bat. When his selfishness was most needed, he was not there.

Bat held aloft, Boycott acknowledges the applause as his home supporters acclaim his 100th century.

GEOFFREY BOYCOTT

Let cricket lovers debate why. When the Yorkshire Achilles eventually stirred from his tent in 1977, an England side which had taken so much punishment from Australia was returning fire. Lillee was absent but Thomson was around. The masterly defensive opener ground out a century on his Test return at Trent Bridge and another, his 100th, at Headingley. In the jubilant afterglow he talked of "my public." Sunset Boulevard had come to the West Riding.

Otherwise affairs at Headingley were unhappy. The relationship between the Grand Old Man and his team-mates became so sour that he was sacked as captain in 1978, and Illingworth was recalled from Leicester. As Illingworth had built a side at Grace Road good enough to win its first championship, and collect four one-day pots, hopes at Yorkshire were high. The native soil was less fertile. Illingworth was confronted by a personality cult around the venerable, and venerated, batsman so strong that normal social intercourse was at times impossible. In their own way, John Hampshire, Chris Old and Bill Athey decided they had had enough, and left.

In the England side the 40-year-old was invigorated by younger men. He led the side briefly, and unsuccessfully, in New Zealand, when Brearley was injured. On Brearley's return in 1981, he again belonged to an England side which regained the Ashes. The last of his 22 Test centuries came against Lillee and Alderman at The Oval. Six months later a Test career which spanned 18 years was over. The circumstances of departure were messy: a valedictory note left on a corkscrew in the dressing room. He was sent home. After 108 Tests and 8,114 runs (then a world record) his time was up. Later that spring he turned up in South Africa, playing for beer (or, in his case, ginseng) money.

Controversy remained a loyal companion. In 1983 he was sacked by Yorkshire yet swam back on a tidal wave of public support not only with a new contract but also as the Wakefield representative of the reconstituted club committee. At an extraordinary meeting in Harrogate the self-styled Reform Group routed the old guard.

His 1984 testimonial produced a club record, £148,000. The following year he scored his 100th century for Yorkshire; the year after, his 150th first-class century. He ended the season eight runs short of 1,000, the first time he had failed to reach that landmark since 1962. It was his final fling; on September 23rd he was sacked, this time for good.

cricket heroes

GEOFFREY BOYCOTT

Things ended painlessly. He was thanked for his efforts by a cricket committee he despised, and on which he has never subsequently served despite offers. For fully 15 months after his dethronement, a year in which Yorkshire won the Benson and Hedges Cup, the Wakefield representative absented himself from club business.

Naturally there was a record to put straight, which he attempted to do in an autobiography, less well-written and certainly less convincing than the book on him by Don Mosey, a one-time acquaintance who was eventually designated a non-person. He prefaced his own book with a line of Thoreau's about marching to different drums. Others suggested Shelley: "Look on my works, ye mighty, and despair".

In his 50th year what can he reflect on? A working life which brought fame and infamy; more runs for England than anyone; more Test centuries than anyone except Hammond and Cowdrey; the support of admirers and the respect of opponents; the passing into popular folklore. Does he now, rich beyond expectation, glimpse, through the post-war mist, the 10-year-old lad who won a Len Hutton bat in a local newspaper competition? How pleased that schoolboy must have been, the world so wonderful and so much to conquer.

Was he free? Was he happy? The question is absurd:
Had anything been wrong we should certainly have heard.

A rare sight as Boycott bowls for England against West Indies.

G. BOYCOTT YORKSHIRE
BORN 21.10.40, FITZWILLIAM, YORKSHIRE

BATTING

	Matches	Innings	Not out	Runs	High score	Avg	100
Test	108	193	23	8,114	246*	47.72	22
First class	609	1,014	162	48,426	261*	56.83	151

BOWLING AND FIELDING

	Runs	Wickets	Avg	5 W/I	10 W/M	BB	Ct	St
Test	382	7	54.57	0	0	3/47	33	0
First class	1,459	45	32.42	0	0	4/14	264	0

MIKE BREARLEY

Scyld Berry

Since no one person has watched over a hundred years of Test cricket, it is impossible to say definitively that so-and-so was the finest captain that England has had. But I will argue that Mike Brearley has been as good as any. In two home series against Australia, in 1977 and 1981, he won three Tests and did not lose one himself. In fact, when Brearley was captain, England went three whole summers without a defeat, quite the reverse of recent years when every Allan, Viv and Imran has won a series in England. If a grey-bearded, silver-haired figure with sloping shoulders stood at first slip and directed the national fortunes, cricket followers could be sure that England would not fail for want of thought.

One must, however, have reservations about every cricketer, because no human being can deal perfectly with every facet of such an intricate game. In Brearley's case, they do not really concern his captaincy, and in only a small measure his batting, although that could be a cause of anxiety — in 1978 for example. Rather, these reservations concern his merits as a selector while England captain, but even these did not arise until the later stages of his career.

Perhaps the wisest move that 'Gubby' Allen made was to back Brearley to cleanse the Middlesex stables, starting in the 1971 season. Brearley had been an outstanding batsman at Cambridge until 1964, scoring over 4,000 runs in four seasons there, but thereafter he had not made as many for Middlesex. He did not play a full season while he was furthering his philosophy in California or lecturing at Newcastle University. The challenge of being a leader, and of purging Middlesex of its discordant characters, was required to tempt him to become a full-time professional.

By 1976 he was established in the 1500 runs-a-year category, and chosen for the England side on batting merit. Against the West Indian fast bowlers, in two Tests that summer, he defended soundly enough to make one think that he was being saved for higher things when he was omitted. Sure enough, he was appointed Tony Greig's vice-captain in India and Australia that winter; and he established himself as an opening batsman, seen to best advantage when wearing the hair shirt of dogged defence — Geoff Boycott then was still in his tent — while a strokeplayer kept the scoreboard moving at the other end.

Mike Brearley — England's most astute captain?

BRIAN CLOSE

Pakistan and was sacked for matters totally unconnected with Test cricket. In his eight years as county captain Yorkshire won the County Championship four times and the Gillette Cup twice, yet he was summarily dismissed.

The plain fact emerges that Close must have been one of the unluckiest cricketers ever. Misfortune and controversy dogged him at every step, each incident in a chequered career accompanied by massive publicity of an unwelcome nature. That is something which happens only to the hugely talented and/or the spectacular, larger-than-life characters of sport as his young friend (and to some extent his protege) Ian Botham was to discover.

That Close was a flawed sporting genius there can be no doubt. For all his 52 centuries, he never made a double hundred. His ability to analyse other players was brilliant but he could never come to terms with his own shortcomings. He had a masterly cricket brain, was (and is) an intelligent man, but showed on many occasions that he lacked simple common sense. He was the toughest of competitors on a sporting field of any kind but there was (and is) no malice in the man. That is why those who have known him all his life sometimes regard his cricket career as a tragedy rather than the triumph it promised to be when he did that first 'double' in 1949.

If that career did not in the end fulfil its earliest potential, Brian Close has at least left behind his philosophy of leadership which cannot in any way be faulted. "Captaincy," he once said, "is all about giving. You have to give something of yourself to every man you play with and all of yourself to the side."

D. B. CLOSE   YORKSHIRE AND SOMERESET
BORN 24.2.31, RAWDON, LEEDS, YORKSHIRE

BATTING

	Matches	Innings	Not out	Runs	High score	Avg	100
Test	22	37	2	887	70	25.34	—
First class	786	1,225	173	34,994	198	33.26	52

BOWLING AND FIELDING

	Runs	Wickets	Avg	5 W/I	10 W/M	BB	Ct	St
Test	532	18	29.55	0	0	4/35	24	0
First class	30,947	1,171	26.42	43	3	8/41	813	1

DENIS COMPTON

Jack Bailey

Compton strides out with Bill Edrich to bat for England. Opposite page: Compton leaves the field at Hastings in 1947 after having made his 17th century of the summer, thus beating Jack Hobbs's 16 centuries of 1925.

Denis Compton was the batting genius of his time. His talent was there for all to recognise, from the very young to the old wiseacres who had long since seen most of everything there was to see, and had been unimpressed by a great deal of that. His brand of batsmanship struck a chord in the same way that Robin Hood did, or Houdini, or Alexander the Great — instantly striking as in a class beyond compare.

We aspiring young cricketers in the late Forties had, I believe, the best view of Denis. He was everything you ever wanted to be — tousled, enjoying a lark, yet the brightest star in a glittering firmament when the dark skies of the war were still a strong and sombre memory.

Playing at the Oval in 1947 for the Young Amateurs of Surrey during the school holiday, the day's play shortened by an early finish, some of us made our way by tube across London, hurrying through the crowds, past the ticket barriers and up and down escalators in the hope of seeing the great man in action during that most famous of all his seasons. It was late August and until then we had been able to follow his exploits only via radio commentary and the pages of the press.

Our brief visit to the free seats at the Nursery End was rewarded by an innings of heroic content and proportions. Middlesex were making a gallant attempt to score 397 runs in the fourth innings for victory. To do so they had to score at 90 runs an hour. The pitch assisted the Kent spinners, Doug Wright, Ray Dovey and Jack Davies, and Middlesex lost their first four wickets for 130 runs. But all this was forgotten as Compton unfurled every stroke in his unique repertoire, smashing into smithereens every semblance of good order in the Kent attack while careering to his thirteenth century of the season, persuading the ball to the boundary nineteen times, making in all 168 runs out of the Middlesex total of 321 and carrying his team within sight of an elusive victory.

This was the golden summer of Compton's eighteen centuries — six of them against the touring South Africans — and 3,816 runs, when the sun shone unremittingly and he broke and remoulded every record for an individual in an English season. It was the flip of a coin as to whose was the best recognised face in England — Compton's, which appeared large on every London

c r i c k e t   h e r o e s

DENIS COMPTON

Transport bus promoting a well-known brand of hair cream, or Cary Grant's, or Winston Churchill's.

I was present when, a week or two later, he made 246 for the Champion County against the Rest at the Oval. Even now I can picture him advancing, tripping, falling and then sweeping Goddard off his nose from a virtually prone position, the ball going for four. It was then confirmed to all small boys what they had long suspected — that he was descended, like Superman, from some distant planet and was possessed of supernatural powers.

In fact, he was born in Hendon on 23rd May, 1918, the son of athletically-minded parents and brother of Leslie. Both brothers played football for Arsenal and England and cricket for Middlesex in the days when professional sportsmen were poorly rewarded financially and fun and good times were the spur.

Denis was 14 years old when he made 85 for North London Schools v South London Schools at Lord's. The following year, he scored 114 against a Public Schools team, again at Lord's — a ground he was to make largely his own. At the age of 17 he was already going in first wicket down for Middlesex. His debut for England came a year later. He had just turned 20 when he played his first innings against Australia and took his first century from the grudging hands of the old enemy.

He went on to a career, interrupted for five prime years by the war, which brought him 38,942 runs and 123 scores of more than a hundred. Nearly 6,000 of his runs came in Test matches. While 1947 was his most bountiful year, he had already outlined the shape of things to come when in 1946 he scored 2,403 runs, including ten centuries — two of them above 200.

That winter, in Australia, he joined the illustrious few who have made a century in each innings of a Test match. It was a series in which England failed to win a match, but it was also notable for the way in which Compton (like Edrich) reminded everyone that he was much more than a plunderer when the going was good. Now his batting included a large measure of courage and a refusal to be beaten by the best attack in the world — Lindwall and Miller high on the list.

Even as 1947 was coming to an end the injury to his knee, a result of his parallel life in football, had begun to trouble him. It was to become a

Anna Neagle, the actress, and Compton at the Empress Hall, London in 1949.

c r i c k e t   h e r o e s

DENIS COMPTON

progressively worrisome problem, restricting the movement up and down the wicket which was such an outstanding feature of his game. By 1949 it had grown worse, but it did not prevent him from taking South Africa by storm in 1948/9 when a prolific tour included 300 runs in as many minutes against N. E. Transvaal.

He was eventually to have a knee-cap removed and to fight a long and courageous battle against his disability, but until his last innings in the first class game in 1964 he remained a source of wonderment and joy to cricket followers the wide world over. He continued to play Test cricket until 1956/7 when even his marvellous relationship with South African Test matches and their crowds and cricketers had to come to an end.

His technique was always one which sought to establish a domination over the bowler so that the poor fellow became incapable of bowling line and length after Compton had been at the wicket a short time. He dictated the length at which the ball arrived with him by bewildering speed of foot. His ability to see the ball early and play it late and his powerful forearms and wrists enabled him constantly to improvise beyond the orthodoxy which was, make no mistake, at the heart of all his batting. The eternal schoolboy in him led to methods which in others would have been fatal — the sweep to whichever ball tickled his palate, the shimmy down the wicket to all but the fastest bowlers. His cover-driving left even the most defensive of fields standing by dint of his timing and his strong wrists. He also made powerful use of the cut and the hook, but seldom chose to play the straight drive, perhaps because it presented too little of a challenge.

Another four runs on the board as Compton keeps the scorers busy.

Challenge was always in the air when he was batting and he communicated his love of it instantly to the waiting, watching crowds. He was also a left-arm bowler of greater ability than he or his batting allowed fully to emerge and his fielding was capable of a brilliance possessed by few. One of life's rare talents, he was and is possessed of great friendliness and charm, instantly beguiling and never forgotten.

c r i c k e t   h e r o e s

DENIS COMPTON

Denis had his lean spells. In 1951/2 in Australia for instance, embattled by his knee, he had a wretched time. But he was possessed of great resilience. Even as late as 1963 it was much in evidence. Playing at Lord's for MCC against Pataudi's Oxford team, in front of a sparse crowd and out of practice, he made nought in the first innings. This followed scores of 0 and 1 in his previous two innings against the undergraduates. "They won't think I could ever bat," he told me.

The following day he arrived not before time, as had been known to happen before, borrowed somebody's bat and went out to do battle. For a time he was all at sea. Then it happened. "Come and watch this," called Charles Cobham from the dressing room balcony. We dropped everything and went to look. The Nawab was having difficulty in placing the field for his slow left arm bowler.

Faced with an offside field of six men, Denis had pierced the cordon three times in one over, once by the aerial route into the Mound Stand. Reinforcements were called up. Now the field was split seven/two. The next ball was pitched on the off-stump, of good length. It went, via the famous sweep, down to the very spot from whence the fielder had just been moved. They knew he could bat, all right.

"Some vague, unpunctual star... " wrote Rupert Brooke in a different context. But as an epitaph to Compton, the cricketer, it just about fits the bill.

Relaxing at home with one of the family pets in 1956, towards the end of an illustrious cricketing career.

D. C. S. COMPTON MIDDLESEX
BORN 23.5.18, HENDON, MIDDLESEX

BATTING

	Matches	Innings	Not out	Runs	High score	Avg	100
Test	78	131	15	5,807	278	50.06	17
First class	515	839	88	38,942	300	51.85	123

BOWLING AND FIELDING

	Runs	Wickets	Avg	5 W/I	10 W/M	BB	Ct	St
Test	1,410	25	56.40	1	0	5/70	49	0
First class	20,074	622	32.27	19	3	7/36	415	0

cricket heroes

DENIS COMPTON

"Some vague, unpunctual star..."

COLIN COWDREY

Ivo Tennant

Michael Colin Cowdrey's life was shaped as soon as he was born. His father, a tea planter whose passion for cricket was heightened by his regard for Marylebone Cricket Club, not only christened his son with its famous initials but, almost simultaneously, had him put down for membership. Had the boy become a golfer, or squash or rackets player — for he had no little talent at each — such a christening would have been seen as misguided, eccentric, even foolish; as it was, he became one of the best known, and best loved, of all cricketers.

In terms of statistics, by which he sets no great yardstick, he was one of England's finest batsmen. He played in more than 100 Test matches, scored more than 7,000 runs at an average of over 40 and scored a century of centuries. Such figures brook no argument; they distinguish him as a player of class from one who is merely proficient. Yet for some, colleagues and critics among them, this was not enough. Technically, they said, he was without peer and without fault; but he was too sensitive a person, too much of a theorist to destroy mediocre bowling. He batted well only when the situation demanded it, when there was a challenge to occupy his fertile mind.

Clearly there was truth in this, although it could be said he never appeared to be destroying bowling since he was not a batsman who had to hit the ball. Rather, he caressed it. Timing was everything. There are no pictures to be seen of Cowdrey executing murderous attacking shots in the manner of Sobers or Botham because he did not play them. Even in one-day cricket, which he did not care for, and which, fortunately for him, he did not have to suffer too often, he was loath to hit across the line.

Cowdrey was that phenomenon beloved by the media — a child prodigy. Even he could not explain the speed at which he developed as a cricketer to the extent that he was not let out of sight by his schoolmasters. He returned from India, his birthplace, at a young age to have the boarding school education that, for one of his middle class background, was taken for granted. The ethos of the prep and public schools he attended has not left him, nor the influence of their head masters. They were the earliest of several strong characters to make an impression upon his introspective being.

Cowdrey at the crease during his first tour of Australia in 1954-55.

c r i c k e t h e r o e s

COLIN COWDREY

He was chosen for the 1st XI at Tonbridge just three weeks after arriving for his first term in 1946, when he was 13 years old. He was playing with boys for whom he was fagging. And he was out first ball. Even so, the young Cowdrey retained his place not only for the next match but for the climax to Tonbridge's season — their traditional encounter with Clifton at Lord's. Suffused with nerves, he scored 75 and 44 and realised then, if he had not before, that this was the game for him.

He made his first appearance for Kent when still a schoolboy, and his first for England when still at Oxford. It was obvious even to the most seasoned professional that Cowdrey possessed exceptional ability. At Scarborough in 1954 he made a century for Gentlemen against Players in the presence of Leonard Hutton, an innings which, more than any other, gained him a place on MCC's 1954-5 tour to Australia.

It was on that tour, the first of six which Cowdrey made to Australia, that he scored his first Test century. It was memorable not just for the fact that he made 102 out of a total of 191, but for the maturity with which the runs were made. This was not the innings of an undergraduate just turned 22; it was that of a craftsman. From then on it was clear that for as long as he cared to play cricket, Cowdrey would be an obvious choice for England.

If, then, his technique was as near to faultless as possible, why did he not score even more heavily than he did? There were certainly times when he pottered around the crease against bowlers who were hardly heard of again. His theorising and quest for new challenges could be attributed to his intellect; his inability or reluctance to realise just how good he was to innate modesty and the ethos of his upbringing. "The quiet style has always seemed to me to be the right way to carry one's talents," he wrote. He was the old-fashioned English gent who did not brag. There was, though, a further reason. His sensitivity was coupled with a tendency to worry which, combined with indecisiveness, were serious drawbacks.

Although he was fortunate with those who influenced or helped him — his father-in-law Stuart Chiesman became both chairman of Kent and his part-time employer — he was not the luckiest of cricketers. Of the 27 Tests in which he captained England, ten were against West Indies and Sobers in his prime. Because he was so manifestly gifted he would not only find the boundary while

COLIN COWDREY

others would play and miss but he would get an edge to a ball which others would not come close to touching. When the captaincy was his, seemingly for keeps, he snapped an achilles tendon in a Sunday slogabout. Illingworth, in many ways his complete opposite, deputised and remained as captain for the tour to Australia the following year, 1970.

Even after he retired, having been consigned in his last seasons to batting too low in the Kent order, his marital break-up received an inordinate amount of publicity. When he reached the summit of his cricketing career in becoming President of MCC he had to undergo a heart by-pass operation, the cause of which was, perhaps, not unrelated to his having to resolve differences between MCC and the Test and County Cricket Board which came to an ugly climax with the resignation of MCC's secretary and treasurer.

Yet it is for his felicitous stroke-play that Cowdrey will be best remembered. He made cricket appear the simplest and the most elegant of all games. It says something about his character — although quite what not even he knows — that his best innings came when, for one reason or another, he did not actually want to play. He cites his century and 97 against Hall and Watson on a lightning fast pitch at Kingston on MCC's 1959-60 tour; his hundred in his hundredth Test against Australia in 1968; and, in almost his last first-class innings, another hundred against them, this time for his beloved Kent. For all his complexities he was a popular person with the general public and was always prepared to find time to talk with them. As a technician, he was the nonpareil.

Batting for Kent against Essex in 1967 after it was announced that he was to lead the team to tour the West Indies later that year.

M. C. COWDREY KENT
BORN 24.12.32, PUTUMALA, INDIA

BATTING

	Matches	Innings	Not out	Runs	High score	Avg	100
Test	114	188	15	7,624	182	44.06	22
First class	692	1,130	134	42,719	307	42.89	107

BOWLING AND FIELDING

	Runs	Wickets	Avg	5 W/I	10 W/M	BB	Ct	St
Test	104	0	0	0	0	0	120	0
First class	3,329	65	51.21	0	0	4/22	638	0

TED DEXTER

John Woodcock

As a striker of the ball, at both cricket and golf, Ted Dexter possessed a wonderful talent. Whether it would have enabled him to become a great golfer we shall never know; but to say that it made him the most imposing figure at the batting crease of any Englishman since Walter Hammond is no exaggeration. If colleagues were sometimes puzzled by his train of thought, with a bat in his hand he left no-one in any doubt as to his intentions. Although an inveterate theorist, he had a method that was classically simple. He stood in the natural way, just as he would have done when he first picked up a bat, and he kept his head still. And when his courage came to be put to the test, against the West Indian fast bowlers, he gave not an inch of ground.

At school Dexter was already mature beyond his years. "How interesting that you have your boys back after their National Service," said a visiting headmaster to the Warden of Radley during a rugger match one day. Dexter had just stormed Radley into the lead. At Cambridge he was soon drawing the crowds to Fenner's — from the ladies' colleges as well as the men's (the sexes were segregated in those days). Cyril Washbrook went back to Old Trafford, after Dexter had scored 185 (105 of them before lunch on the first day) for the University against Lancashire, saying that never before had he had to field such stinging drives at cover point as from some aloof young undergraduate they were calling 'Lord Edward'.

Until railway sleepers began to be used as bats, the ball can never have been hit any harder than by Dexter. He was six feet tall and very strong with a natural sense of timing, and a full swing. I can see him now, driving an off break from Tom Veivers for six on the Melbourne Cricket Ground, the ball only just clearing the sightscreen yet still on its way up as it did so. It really was going like a rocket.

This was on Dexter's second tour of Australia — in 1962-63 when he was captain. His first, under Peter May four years earlier, had been a disappointment, though that was not entirely his own fault. Had the selectors delayed choosing May's side until after the Fourth Test Match against New Zealand in July 1958, Dexter would probably have been in the original party. Instead they picked it on the Sunday, and on the Monday Dexter, having been

TED DEXTER

left out, made 52 in his first innings for England. When, eventually, he was flown out as a replacement, he remained somewhat isolated.

Communication was no more May's forte than Dexter's, and things were already going badly on the field by the time Dexter arrived. Besides Alan Davidson's late and unpredictable swing and Richie Benaud's probing spin, England had to contend with a raging epidemic of Australian throwing. Not until the tour moved on to New Zealand was Dexter seen in his true colours. The Australians had unnerved him. In New Zealand the chance to recover his confidence was gratefully, and mercifully, accepted. I say mercifully because of the style he was to bring to the game.

His next Test hundred, the following winter, was in Barbados, at the start of his only tour of the West Indies. Although he was still only 24 the West Indian fast bowlers brought the best out in him, as they did in England four years later when his 70 in 73 balls in the Lord's Test, after England had been 20 for two in their first innings, constituted the perfect response to a crisis.

Playing with the disdain for bowlers which his batting conveyed was not always to his advantage. Twenty-seven times in Tests he passed 50 without going on to get a hundred, which could be said to have been rather careless of him. When he did put his mind to it he could filibuster with the best of them. Against Pakistan at Karachi, for example, in 1961-62 he was eight and a half hours making 205, while at Old Trafford in 1964, when Australia had left England with only a draw to play for, he batted eight hours for 174.

Dexter had four full series as England's captain, taking MCC on a combined tour of India and Pakistan in 1961-62 and to Australia in 1962-63, and leading England at home against West Indies in 1963 and Australia in 1964. The chances are that he would have had charge in South Africa too, in 1964-65, had he not been unavailable for the start of that tour through contesting the constituency of Cardiff South-East in the General Election of 1964. His opponent in a straight fight, Jim Callaghan, was on his way to becoming Prime Minister, and although Dexter was a distant outsider at Cardiff he could hardly have been appointed captain of a cricket side that left for Rhodesia on polling day. In the event, the score was Callaghan, Leonard James (Labour) 30,129; Dexter, Edward Ralph (Conservative) 22,288, and in South Africa Dexter played under M. J. K. Smith.

c r i c k e t   h e r o e s

TED DEXTER

TED DEXTER

Dexter came out of retirement to play for the Duke of Norfolk's XI against Australia at Arundel in 1972

Of Dexter's 31 Tests as captain, ten were won, seven lost and fourteen drawn. Of the victories, five were against Pakistan, in the days when they travelled badly, and three against New Zealand. In that he found it hard to tune in to the ordinary mortal, or for that matter to stay in regular contact with events on the field, he fitted into no conventional category as a captain. Such, though, was his flair for the game — with the ball as well as the bat — and his indifference to criticism, that solecisms tended to be passed over. With the 16th Duke of Norfolk as Dexter's manager, MCC were represented in Australia in 1962-63 by a uniquely seigneurial pair.

Dexter's retirement in 1965, when he was only just 30, seemed sadly premature, as he had so much left to give. No doubt the independent streak that he had in him, as well as a certain restlessness, had something to do with it, and, although the distinction between amateur and professional had ended, cricket had yet to provide the sort of living he could make elsewhere. A broken leg, suffered when he was pushing his car to safety after running out of petrol, was another factor. Persuaded to reappear for a few matches for Sussex in 1968 (he had captained them from 1960 to 1965), Dexter began with an innings of 203 not out at Hastings on July 20th and was back in the England side against Australia a week later.

For 50 years I have watched the great cricketers of the world in action, and for sheer ability Ted Dexter has to rank very high among them. After Hampshire had won their first county championship in 1961 I asked Roy Marshall, perhaps the best white West Indian batsman there has ever been, how many *unplayable* balls had dismissed him that season. "Only one," he said, "and that was from Dexter at Portsmouth." When Gary Player had a round of golf with Dexter at Adelaide in 1962 he could scarcely believe his eyes, so splendid was Dexter's striking of the ball. If Severiano Ballesteros had been a cricketer, I think he would have played the game much as Dexter did — by impulse one moment and instinct the next, sometimes with circumspection and regularly with the sort of dash that is not easily forgotten.

With it all, Dexter has been thorough-going. He could not otherwise have become, in quite a short time, skilled enough as a pilot to fly himself, his wife and their two children from England to Australia in a six-seater Piper Aztec, to report, for the *Sunday Mirror*, the MCC tour of 1970-71. There is, I am sure,

TED DEXTER

something of the pioneer in him, as well as of the puritan and the politician; he is both perfectionist and punter.

In his time he has mounted the pulpit to preach the gospel, bred greyhounds to win good races, devoured the *Sporting Life*, defied convention, seldom countenanced compromise, starred at athletics, excelled at rackets, owned the grandest of cars and the mightiest of motor bikes, holed the Old Course at Sunningdale in 63 strokes (the first nine holes in 29), hit the ball out of the Adelaide Oval, been as cavalier as a young man as, in due time, he grew to be congenial, and admitted to no mistakes after a disastrous first season as Chairman of the England Cricket Committee. As a batsman, even the Australians came to hold him in awe; that can be said of very few, and it is a measure of his game.

E. R. DEXTER SUSSEX
BORN 15.5.35, MILAN, ITALY

BATTING

	Matches	Innings	Not out	Runs	High score	Avg	100
Test	62	102	8	4,502	205	47.89	9
First class	327	567	48	21,150	205	40.75	51

BOWLING AND FIELDING

	Runs	Wickets	Avg	5 W/I	10 W/M	BB	Ct	St
Test	2,306	66	34.93	0	0	4/10	29	0
First class	12,539	419	29.92	9	2	7/24	234	0

BASIL d'OLIVEIRA

Robin Marlar

Single-handedly Basil d'Oliveira killed off the notion that politics and sport could be kept apart. Whether they should be regarded as separate and inviolate compartments in life's locker is another matter. To many, the plea that sport be left alone was always simplistic, and therefore an appropriate plank on which stupid sportsmen, with their brains in their feet, could base a self-centred philosophy. The recent history of international sport has shown that sport is an irresistibly easy target for politicians, whose power is all-pervading. Two wrecked Olympic Games and cricket's long struggle to hammer out a formula for its involvement with d'Oliveira's country of origin, South Africa, are obvious examples of sport's frailty when the politicians start to lean.

When John Vorster, then the grandly-titled State President of South Africa, had decided that 'Dolly', as he was already universally known, a socially classified coloured from the ironically-named Cape of Good Hope, could not be accepted in the land of his birth as a touring member of an MCC team, another principle came into play. In all sport involving international competition the visiting party must be chosen without pressure from the host country, whether that pressure be sporting or political. MCC cancelled the tour and, in cricket at least, South Africa's isolation had effectively begun.

It is a curious fact that in the final stages of cricket's resolution of the South African problem, action by politicians against the principle of unfettered selection proved the trigger for an acceptable compromise. By deploying the politicians' superior power over right of entry, the Indian Government's threat wrecked an England cricket tour, and it was the prospect of endless chaos to their international programme which persuaded cricket's leaders to devise a settlement of the South African issue which was acceptable to all the governments involved. By refusing to bend before the Indian Government's threat, preferring to cancel the tour, England's cricket held fast to the honourable tradition of rejecting direct government interference in selection which began with the d'Oliveira affair.

With the perspective of a quarter of a century we can see clearly how an extrovert, popular player came to be elevated like a totem, a rallying point for the disadvantaged and the oppressed, to such an extent that he became a

Opposite page: Basil d'Oliveira, playing for MCC, despatches a ball from Yorkshire's Brian Close at Lord's in 1968.

cricket heroes

BASIL d'OLIVEIRA

legend even before the onset of middle age. To his thousands of friends Basil d'Oliveira remained wonderfully unaffected by his status as a towering figure in sporting history as he played out his career first as a cricketer, then as a coach, and always as a good companion — albeit one a little dangerous in the small hours of the next morning.

Of course, the South African Government took all the blame and South African sport suffered all the consequences of the row. No doubt there would have been other incidents involving other sportsmen which would have sent South Africa into sporting isolation. The truth of the matter is, however, that the principal responsibility for provoking the d'Oliveira affair lay not with the South African Government or Prime Minister but with England's cricket selectors, who perpetuated yet another example of ineptitude by omitting d'Oliveira from the original selection of the team. When he was subsequently inserted as a replacement, the South African politicians naturally smelt a rat, believing, with some justification, that far from politics interfering with sport, here was an

d'Oliveira and Tom Graveney, left, on the way to the wicket to resume the batting against West Indies in the Old Trafford Test Match of 1969.

example — an intolerable example — of sport seeking to interfere with politics. The ban on Dolly was not so much an action as a reaction on the part of John Vorster.

No-one has yet completely unravelled the d'Oliveira affair. British politicians and diplomats with fine cricketing pedigrees such as Sir Alec Douglas-Home and Lord Cobham, both class county players and later presidents of the MCC, became involved. There was much discussion before and after about the acceptability of coloured, or indeed black, sportsmen in South Africa — where petty apartheid was rampant then more than now, so much so that blacks were allowed in hotels only as staff. In the end Vorster said that South Africa would not accept a team forced upon her by those with "certain political aims". Few

BASIL d'OLIVEIRA

in England accepted the word of the selectors that they were totally unfettered by such considerations and free to choose whom they would. Amongst those who believed the selectors was the Archbishop of Canterbury!

They were, and still are, to be believed. "By their ineptitude shall they be known," is a standing jibe against England's cricket selectors. 1968 was not one of their best summers. They gathered a huge squad together at Old Trafford, including Dolly — who made 87 not out in England's second innings and took a wicket in each Australian innings — but when Ken Barrington pulled out England fielded only three front-line bowlers and were beaten. The next three Tests were drawn and Dolly appeared as a hunch selection for the last Test only because Roger Prideaux, an opening batsman, withdrew on the morning of the match. d'Oliveira made 158 in the first innings, and in the final session took the crucial wicket as Australia battled for the draw. England won and squared a series that should, on paper, have been a doddle for them.

Immediately afterwards the touring team was announced and d'Oliveira's name was not in the party. His omission was received with outrage. Tony Pawson, then cricket correspondent of *The Observer*, wrote one of his finest pieces, attacking the selectors for their lack of gratitude in not acknowledging Dolly's right to be there in the party as the man who had saved England's selectors from red faces. In the eyes of the general public, Pawson thought, they would not be forgiven. Nor were they. At that time I was doing a lot of cricket for BBC News and I remember having to telephone Billy Griffith, a dear friend, who was at that time — when there was no split between the MCC and the TCCB — the Secretary at Lord's, to ask him why this had happened and whether those concerned appreciated the enormity of what they had done. He had toured South Africa as a player and was an unhappy man, realising that there would be an outcry. Thanks to that opportunity to broadcast, my enraged reaction was one of the first. Faced by universal condemnation, the selectors then perpetuated a second chapter of folly. Tom Cartwright, a seam bowler of uniquely unusual merit, pulled out and, surprise, surprise, Basil d'Oliveira, a batting all-rounder, was then chosen as a replacement. Cartwright had been unfit when the team was originally picked! In *Wisden*, Michael Melford, as fair and rational a commentator as cricket has ever known, recorded the statement

BASIL d'OLIVEIRA

d'Oliveira on his way to 50 not out in the second innings of the 1972 Trent Bridge Test against Australia.

by Doug Insole, then chairman of the selectors, that the balance of the side had to be reviewed following Cartwright's withdrawal, and hence the selection of d'Oliveira, who had only been regarded as a batsman. No rational defence could, however, assuage public opinion either in England or South Africa. The look of the thing was wrong and everyone knew it, saw it, and understood, bar the selectors.

Theories cannot be tested *post facto* but it remains my conviction that d'Oliveira would have been admitted into South Africa had he been selected, as he should have been, at the outset. Had he been ignored thereafter, as he also should have been, at least that tour would have gone into the record books.

At that time d'Oliveira was 34. Two years earlier he had been nominated as one of *Wisden's* five Cricketers of the Year, the cricketers' special accolade. So this cricketing dispute was not about an inconsequential player. True, 1968 was a patchy summer for him, but the talent was obvious and he was to feature in England teams for another three years.

Because of his prowess at cricket, d'Oliveira's progress was rags to relative riches on an international scale. He was playing in the league organised by the South African Cricket Board and breaking all records. Not that you could find him mentioned at that time in the pages of *Wisden*. This was a league restricted to Cape coloureds who could watch cricket at the beautiful Newlands ground but not play there.

Hassan Howa, the campaigning secretary of the SACB, used to say that there were plenty more members of his flock as good as Dolly. Others were certain that he was the best and tried their utmost to get him to England as a teenager. They failed. He was working as a printing machine operator in Cape Town when he finally secured a contract with the Middleton club in Lancashire. John Arlott, the great commentator, promoted his application. Once there he began to score heavily and take wickets so often that he was chosen for a Commonwealth side. Tom Graveney talked his team-mate into a career in county cricket and Worcestershire eventually got the d'Oliveira signature ahead of Lancashire and Gloucestershire.

As a batsman he was, above all, correct. Most players brought up on bad wickets have to understand technique. His particular strength was in his

BASIL d'OLIVEIRA

forearms and as a straight six-hitter with minimum apparent effort. That memory of Dolly remains vivid to this day. He was, on most days, a fine fielder anywhere and was important at that time as a slip catcher. His bowling action was rather special. As a natural medium pacer he was one of the rare breed of bowlers who, in their final stride, bring one foot — in his case the right — up alongside the other before delivery takes place. In coaching such rarities are known as "clickers". He had variation of pace and a natural ability to move the ball in from the offside.

These manifold cricketing gifts, this all-round competence, have furnished Basil d'Oliveira with both the knowledge and the confidence to become a fine teacher of the game. Worcestershire's many successes during the 1980s have been largely due to the capability of locally-matured players to give the team a form of inner strength to support the deeds of the county's star players. Even the great Graeme Hick has had cause to be grateful for Dolly's ability to identify bad habits and thus encourage a return to basic technique.

Who knows what the spring of that inner strength may be? Could it be an outflow from a whole lake of experience which only Dolly can know and which even he cannot communicate — even if he wished to? The escape from coloured status, recognition in another land and the huge weight of public exposure as the central figure in an international scandal are experiences given to few. Dolly has survived with his pride and integrity intact, and he remains a good mate to millions. His is quite a story.

B. L. d'OLIVEIRA WORCESTERSHIRE
BORN 4.10.31, CAPE TOWN, SOUTH AFRICA

BATTING

	Matches	Innings	Not out	Runs	High score	Avg	100
Test	44	70	8	2,484	158	40.06	5
First class	362	566	88	18,919	227	39.57	43

BOWLING AND FIELDING

	Runs	Wickets	Avg	5 W/I	10 W/M	BB	Ct	St
Test	1,859	47	39.55	0	0	3/46	29	0
First class	15,021	548	27.41	17	2	6/29	211	0

c r i c k e t   h e r o e s

GODFREY EVANS

He played his first game for Kent in 1939, as a batsman, and his last in 1967, eight years after he had officially retired. Of his 1,066 first-class victims 250 were stumped, a lower percentage than Leslie Ames, his predecessor (703 catches, 418 stumpings), but higher than Alan Knott, his successor (1,211 catches, 133 stumpings). For all but 60 years the three of them brought their own very special glitter to the grounds of Kent. With the bat Evans's best season was 1952, when he scored 1,613 runs (average 28.80).

Now, many years on, he is almost completely hidden behind a dense clump of whiskers. He is still instantly recognisable, all the same, by his brisk step and trim but thick-set figure, as he makes for the press box with the latest set of prices on the current match. If the bookmakers who use his services had operated in his own day, they would have had to offer longish odds against his allowing a bye. In 1946-47 in successive Australian innings of 659 for eight and 365 there were none.

Evans claims another victim for Kent in 1957.

T. G. EVANS KENT
BORN 18.8.20, FINCHLEY, MIDDLESEX

BATTING

	Matches	Innings	Not out	Runs	High score	Avg	100
Test	91	133	14	2,439	104	20.49	2
First class	465	753	52	14,882	144	21.22	7

BOWLING AND FIELDING

	Runs	Wickets	Avg	5 W/I	10 W/M	BB	Ct	St
Test	0	0	0	0	0	—	173	46
First class	245	2	122.50	0	0	2/50	816	250

c r i c k e t   h e r o e s

C.B.FRY

Alan Ross

"Fry could, alike in form and in feature, have stepped straight out of the frieze of the Parthenon." So wrote H. S. Altham, who, in the same article, remarked: "Fry was beyond all doubt the greatest all-round athlete, and one of the most gifted men, that ever played cricket for England." Photographs confirm the first statement; the second goes without saying.

Around the turn of the century Fry's athletic feats were among the wonders of the age: world record long jump holder, four years in the Repton and Oxford XIs and captain of both, a soccer international who played for Southampton in the F. A. Cup Final of 1902, captain of Sussex 1904-8 and England in 1912.

Fry averaged 50 in a career that lasted from 1894 to 1921. In 1901 he hit 13 hundreds, six in succession, his total runs for the season being 3,147. For England he averaged only 31, but, as Denzil Batchelor points out in his elegant essay on Fry, that was only one run less than Victor Trumper's average and better than those of J. T. Tyldesley, Braund, or M. A. Noble.

Fry was many things besides a notable sportsman: a classicist at Oxford second only to the great F. E. Smith, a successful author and journalist, an adviser to the Maharajah Jam Sahib of Nawanagar (Ranji) at the League of Nations in Geneva. He was, in his golden youth — when in addition to the feats listed above, he acquired fame as rugby player, sprinter and high jumper — a man of all the talents, with the world apparently at his feet. The slight mystery at the heart of Fry's life is that, despite all these gifts of scholarship and athleticism, he settled for life in a comparative backwater, for 50 years nominal head of a training ship that in fact was run by his energetic and formidable wife.

Fry's marriage was an odd affair. His wife Beatie was 36, ten years older than Fry, when they married. Beatie already had two illegitimate children by Charles Hoare, a banker, and for some years after her marriage to Fry, Beatie moved between the two of them. It was Hoare who bought the training ship Mercury, which, after his death, went to the Frys and which Beatie ruled with a rod of iron. Fry's autobiography *Life Worth Living* has many virtues, but it tells nothing of his married life, omits all reference to the appalling nervous breakdown he suffered in 1929 and which lasted five years, and fails to

C . B . F R Y

mention his numerous efforts to become a Liberal Member of Parliament. On the other hand, the book retains through several editions an account of Fry's 1934 meeting with Hitler and his undisguised admiration for the Nazi philosophy. What was it about this intellectual grandee that made him so naive about contemporary events, that despite his devotion to the classics made him so ignorant about the art and literature of his time?

In the nets in 1921, at the end of a long and astounding sports career.

There are several possibilities, the most likely being the vaunted classical education, which set him in his own mind above others and whose golden age made the present, in his eyes, of little account. For all his qualifications, Fry was so insensitive to others that he was never elected to the committee of MCC and never kept a publisher or editor for long. Reading *Life Worth Living* you get no idea of his vulnerabilities or failures, which is a pity because it would have made him seem so much more human. Instead, the book gives off an air of serenity and well-being, of comparatively small-time public success. Fry described his detailed knowledge about the workings of cars and wireless waves, his skill and devotion to dancing, but nothing about the workings of his own mind or heart.

"Cricket was a dance with a bat in your hand," Fry observed once. Yet, curiously, this Apollo, with the world at his feet, was the least dancing of cricketers. In their great partnership over the years for Sussex it was Ranji who was the natural dancer, Fry the student who had to learn the steps. And Fry did learn. He may have wished at various stages of his life to be remembered as something other than a cricketer, but it is as a cricketer more than anything else that he lays claim to our attention.

The master of back and on-side play, Fry studied the arts and techniques of batting with the same thoroughness he devoted to engines and radio. He may, to some eyes, always have seemed a manufactured player, but if so his figures point to an extraordinary mastery of his subject. Fry hit 94 hundreds, 16

C . B . FRY

double hundreds, two Test hundreds. In later life he talked the hindlegs off all and sundry, and with his monocle and chauffeur-driven Bentley, his champagne and air of effortless superiority, was not to everyone's taste. His high-handedness cost him many friends but at the wicket there was nobody to take offence.

C. B. FRY   SURREY, SUSSEX AND HAMPSHIRE
BORN 25.4.1872, WEST CROYDON, SURREY

BATTING

	Matches	Innings	Not out	Runs	High score	Avg	100
Test	26	41	3	1,223	144	32.18	2
First class	394	658	43	30,886	258*	50.22	94

BOWLING AND FIELDING

	Runs	Wickets	Avg	5 W/I	10 W/M	BB	Ct	St
Test	3	0	0	0	0	—	17	0
First class	4,872	166	29.34	9	2	6/78	240	0

cricket heroes

HAROLD GIMBLETT

David Foot

I grew up believing Harold Gimblett was a more sublime batsman than Bradman. His maiden hundred, in 63 minutes at unpretentious Frome, was enshrined in West Country culture. I was just six when he missed the bus and hitched his way to the ground for the most romantic of all cricketing baptisms. In no time, along with most of my other friends around the villages of Somerset, I was able — without changing a word of the narrative — to recite the vagaries of Harold's journey to Frome and the subsequent sequence of strokes he made with Wellard's borrowed bat.

In the years that followed I took the single-track train to Taunton on half-terms and Bank Holidays. Sometimes Gloucestershire were the visitors. I don't remember Hammond from those days; I can recall virtually every cover drive from Gimblett. Indeed I made a point of sitting on the grass where I knew, at least once, I should be able to push aside my sandwich box and field the ball.

Gimblett's maiden 100 was made in only 63 minutes — with a borrowed bat!

We all went just to see him. That wasn't to belittle the pace of Andrews and Wellard in tandem, the delicate efficiency of Luckes behind the stumps, the comfortable waddle up to the wickets of Hazell, the quaint, stuttering run and protruding bottom of Buse. There were greater extroverts than Gimblett, more amusing fellows. But he, in that often mysterious way in which an affinity is established between a sportsman and a crowd, was our unchallenged hero.

In retrospect, it's hard to analyse exactly why. He carried a gloomy, occasionally preoccupied, expression. He didn't throw himself about in the field — though I can't remember him ever dropping a catch or being inaccurate with that powerful underarm return — and seldom betrayed even a flicker of a smile. But, just like the farmers across the road in the market, we dropped everything when Gimblett was going to the wicket. He engendered the hustle of expectancy at Taunton, Bath and Weston (or Frome) just as Viv Richards was to do forty years later.

What thrilled us about Gimblett was his contempt for batting ritual. Like Gloucestershire's Charlie Barnett — although he belonged to an alien county and lacked comparable appreciation among the Somerset schoolboys — Harold batted with instinctive relish. He considered it his right to dispatch two half volleys in the first over. His first shot was often a straight drive which hit the

c r i c k e t   h e r o e s

HAROLD GIMBLETT

sight-screen first bounce. Once, against Hampshire, he hooked three times to the long-leg boundary, as if arrogantly demolishing a Southampton-based theory tried out at the outset to test his supposed vulnerability.

Lord's advised him to cut out the hook shot, it is true. "Stuff them!" was his normal retort. In fact, he became needlessly paranoiac about the game's inner

Gimblett on his way to another century for Somerset, this time against Surrey at the Oval in 1951.

sanctum and the aristocrats of the Long Room. No player had more complexes. Harold had been to a minor public school in North Devon. He had social graces and a nice speaking voice. Maybe, with a kind of inverted snobbery, he felt he should have done better with his life than be a relatively poorly paid professional cricketer in a county where, according to him, half the committee didn't know anything about the game and there was too much of an ex-military presence.

He bristled when he went to Lord's and was inclined to be brusque with those in authority. MCC members were to him "puffed-up buffoons in those tomato-and-egg ties." He used to tell me he was always being slighted and denied his right, as a former Test player, simply to stand in the Long Room. Privilege angered him, in any guise. He came from Conservative farming stock but his politics wavered towards the left. He worried incessantly — about what he saw as lack of money for his wife and himself in old age, about his health, about declining standards in society, about greedy landlords: a mixed bag of neuroses.

The irony is that he created so much joy. He scored 49 hundreds for his county and one for the Commonwealth XI. He played three times for England and would have gone to India but for the war. There was a later summons for the Trent Bridge Test against the West Indians in 1950. The idea was for him to take over from the injured Hutton and to get after Ramadhin and Valentine. A nation approved. He suddenly developed a carbuncle whose throbbing, untimely presence was avidly charted in all the public prints except *The Lancet*. Many of us believe it was a psychosomatic illness.

c r i c k e t   h e r o e s

HAROLD GIMBLETT

Batting came easy for Harold. He could score runs quite beautifully — and quickly. The timing was exquisite; he could bring out a cover drive to match Hammond's. For years he carried the Somerset batting on those countryman's shoulders. Alas, he lacked the mental fibre to do this. If, as we have said, batting came for the most part easily for him, life itself didn't. He had nervous breakdowns and went to hospital for treatment. Within the dressing room he would be morose and inconsolable after a bad run. In the end he just couldn't cope any longer. He left Somerset quite dramatically, but life after cricket tormented him almost as much. Severe arthritis added to his turmoil. The 'demons' caused him to hate increasingly the game he had adorned with such bravura. He moved impetuously into a mobile home in the New Forest to get right away from the Somerset supporters who just wanted to talk cricket. In March 1978, at the time of year when he still unfailingly thought of pre-season nets, he took his life. He was only 63.

It filled us all with regrets and even guilt. We'd basked in the manner of his 23,000 runs and his 300 at Eastbourne. We'd loved him in spite of his moods. We'd tolerated his regular harangues, directed sometimes unreasonably at county officials and cricket's rulers. Maybe we should have tried harder to understand. In one spell of depression, he told me: "What I needed was more friends in cricket. Like that lovely bloke who showed me with his umbrella the way to play inswing after my Test flop at Lord's. His name was Jack Hobbs and I went out and made 67 in the second innings." It was one of the few times I saw my idol smile.

H. GIMBLETT SOMERSET
BORN 19.10.14, BICKNOLLER, SOMERESET

BATTING

	Matches	Innings	Not out	Runs	High score	Avg	100
Test	3	5	1	129	67*	32.25	0
First class	368	673	37	23,007	310	36.17	50

BOWLING AND FIELDING

	Runs	Wickets	Avg	5 W/I	10 W/M	BB	Ct	St
Test	0	0	0	0	0	—	1	0
First class	2,124	41	51.80	0	0	4/10	247	0

c r i c k e t   h e r o e s

DAVID GOWER

Alan Lee

For those of us whose cricket careers have been dignified by nothing grander than the occasional painstaking 50, nudged and nicked against the rustic bowling of some remote village side, David Gower has offered pain as well as pleasure. Is it fair, we ask ourselves, that this gifted young man can find the complex art of batting so absurdly simple and can sail through the pressurised lifestyle of the modern international cricketer with no weightier concerns than the venue for his evening meal? The answer, of course, is that he cannot and does not.

Gower is every bit as misunderstood as his fellow England captain, Graham Gooch. But, while Gooch's qualities are submerged beneath a public front popularly considered solemn at best and surly at worst, Gower is widely thought to be glib, nerveless and utterly natural when, in point of fact, he is nothing of the kind.

David Gower deep in thought during the 1986 West Indies tour.

He has, it must be admitted, committed various acts over the years which have done nothing to dispel the illusion of a modern-day cavalier. Pulling his first ball in Test cricket for four with patronising precision reinforced the myth that he finds the game all too easy; scorning a net practice to go windsurfing after his own England side had lost to an island team in the Caribbean perpetuated the notion of a casual, even careless personality. I know for a fact that he regrets the windsurfing affair; I have an idea that he would also prefer it if people did not draw quite so many conclusions from that indolent stroke at Edgbaston back in 1978. For, if there have been times when David has been amused by his public image, he has increasingly come to wish that the man in the street knew a little more of the truth.

The truth, Gower style, is the story of a man with a God-given talent to play cricket and a self-imposed commitment to the quality of life. He has never, personally, considered the two to be mutually exclusive and neither, to my knowledge, has he allowed the self-indulgences of the latter to distort the ambitions of the former. Others, however, have judged the matter more harshly and it is perhaps because of this that David Gower reached the end of the 1980s, aged 32 and ostensibly at his peak, with his future in the game clouded in uncertainty and tainted by understandable disillusionment.

c r i c k e t   h e r o e s

DAVID GOWER

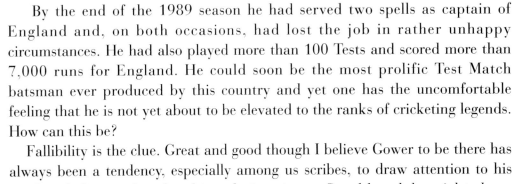

By the end of the 1989 season he had served two spells as captain of England and, on both occasions, had lost the job in rather unhappy circumstances. He had also played more than 100 Tests and scored more than 7,000 runs for England. He could soon be the most prolific Test Match batsman ever produced by this country and yet one has the uncomfortable feeling that he is not yet about to be elevated to the ranks of cricketing legends. How can this be?

Fallibility is the clue. Great and good though I believe Gower to be there has always been a tendency, especially among us scribes, to draw attention to his niggling failings rather than his enduring virtues. So, although he might play a dozen glorious off-side strokes during an innings, we still chide him for the instinctive dart which has him caught by one of two posted gullies. Or, he might force the ball square on the legside with impeccable timing during a first-innings century yet fail to escape censure for being caught behind in the second through not getting enough bat on the shot

This frustrates him more than he indicates, for the simple reason that he cares about his performances, and about people's perception of them. While he is enviably capable of compartmentalising his life, even he cannot walk off the field and forget — nor would he want to.

A convivial companion — witty and intelligent — Gower is, however, some distance from being the iceberg many people imagine. He has nerves, and they are known to jangle quite severely on the big occasion. He also has a temper, and those who have played under him both for Leicestershire and England will testify to the short fuse which can blow if he feels he is having to suffer fools. Somehow, the warts are endearing, the awareness of mortal weaknesses comforting. They mean that Gower can and must be judged in the same way as everyone else, not as some superior being whose every slip must be microscopically examined. Look at him this way and his right to a place among the game's legends is indisputable.

He kicked off his county career with Leicestershire at the age of 18. His apprenticeship was served under Ray Illingworth, who, although sometimes exasperated by the less serious side of the Gower nature, recognised a rare talent and did as much as anyone to nurture it. Jack Birkenshaw, another early team-mate and another Yorkshireman, joins Illingworth among those whose

Perfect balance from Gower as he shows once again why he is regarded as one of cricket's greatest ever left-handers.

DAVID GOWER

advice Gower respected. They helped make him an England player by the age of 21, not just in name but in maturity. He could handle Test cricket in a fashion few so young could hope to do. It was inevitable he would go on to captain England and almost as inevitable that the affair would end in tears. Gower never could see eye to eye with Peter May, then chairman of selectors, and although he won two series as captain, his sacking was messy. Three years on, he was reappointed by Ted Dexter amid a fanfare for a new and exciting age. Sadly, England lost 4 - 0 to Australia, the partnership was terminated and Gower was then dropped.

Whatever may lie in the future for the one whose golden curls have now turned a distinguished grey, the past is full of memories. He has played some of the most vividly exciting innings I have ever seen but, out of cast character, also some of the bravest under duress. I think of his match-saving 154 not out against the West Indian pace battery at Kingston in 1981 and, more recently, of his 106 at Lord's in 1989 on the day when his credentials for captaincy were first being queried.

Gower is a man of diverse tastes, a man cricket cannot hope to own for too long. But for as long as he is around we should enjoy him, for he is a sportsman of unusual flair, style and dignity. We could do with more of his sort.

The Oval 1985 and Gower holds aloft the Ashes as England win the six-match series against the Australians.

D. I. GOWER LEICESTERSHIRE
BORN 1.4.57, TUNBRIDGE WELLS, KENT

BATTING

	Matches	Innings	Not out	Runs	High score	Avg	100
Test	106	183	13	7,383	215	43.42	15
First class	358	576	51	20,991	228	39.98	43

BOWLING AND FIELDING

	Runs	Wickets	Avg	5 W/I	10 W/M	BB	Ct	St
Test	20	1	20.00	0	0	1/1	72	0
First class	223	4	55.75	0	0	3/47	222	0

c r i c k e t   h e r o e s

W. G. GRACE

E. W. Swanton

NO. 27.—DR. W. G. GRACE, F.O.S.

It could reasonably be argued that more words have been written about the subject of this sketch than about any Englishman of his time and beyond. It is obviously so of any sportsman. A Bibliography of Cricket lists forty books written about him, or by him — in the latter case the work having been done by another, although in close collaboration. Of this we have evidence in the MCC library in the shape of *Cricket* published under his name in 1891 and written in its entirety in his own firm, legible hand.

In other words there is nothing new to reveal about this phenomenal man who in the time-honoured phrase found cricket a country pastime and left it a national institution. Indeed W. G. Grace, the best-known man in England — coupled according to taste with the Prince of Wales or Mr Gladstone — was himself a national institution, the country doctor, the departure of whose train from Padddington to Bristol, with silk-hatted station-master in attendance, used to await his pleasure. Three-quarters of a century on there can scarcely be a soul alive with any conscious memory of him; yet what initials today are remotely as identifiable with a man as W. G.?

This uniquely powerful public exposure from youth up was partly an accident of time. W. G. was born in 1848, and he burst on to the cricket scene at a time when this game which had been played for centuries by the villagers of the home counties had now also become the diversion of the nobility and gentry. The coming of the railways was exporting it country-wide as well as bringing its devotees to Lord's Ground at St. John's Wood and to Surrey's Kennington Oval. The growth of cricket at the public schools brought about a proliferation of clubs, both resident and wandering. County rivalries were taking shape. Into this scene came the comely son of a Gloucestershire doctor who emerged from the parental orchard and the keen tutelage therein of father, uncle, cousin and — not least — mother, to make, a little before his 16th birthday, a precocious 50 at Lord's against MCC. A year later, in 1865, he played the first two of his 85 matches for the Gentlemen, at the Oval and Lord's.

Precocity is really too mild a word to describe his youthful rise to fame. At the age of 18 he played two innings at the Oval which, Sydney Pardon wrote,

c r i c k e t   h e r o e s

LORD HAWKE

Tests, captaining them in four — all at a time when travelling anywhere would be considered a real hardship by modern standards.

When in England he would always try to get home in order to accompany his mother to church on Sunday. Warner remembered him for passing on what Hawke considered as the "two essentials in choosing an eleven" — good temper and good manners.

He was simultaneously both President and captain of Yorkshire and was instrumental in taking the selection of England teams from the Test ground authority to MCC; he went on to become chairman of selectors and President of MCC.

As to his infamous dictum on professionals I quote from *The Official History of Yorkshire CCC*: "In 1925 when Cec Parkin, in a newspaper, attacked Gilligan's captaincy of England in Australia, Hawke told Yorkshire's AGM: 'Pray God no professional shall ever captain England. I love and admire them all but we have always had an amateur Skipper and when the day comes when we shall have no more amateurs captaining England it shall be a thousand pities.' "

It is perhaps easier to understand, if not agree with, such sentiments now than it was then. Professional captaincy has now ruled long enough for fair comparisons to be made with a system that, while growing rapidly obsolete, was not without its virtues. Hawke knew his Gentlemen and his Players; he also knew his players and his gentlemen.

M. B. (LORD) HAWKE YORKSHIRE
BORN 16.8.1860, GAINSBOROUGH, LINCOLNSHIRE

BATTING

	Matches	Innings	Not out	Runs	High score	Avg	100
Test	5	8	1	55	30	7.85	0
First class	633	936	105	16,749	166	20.15	13

BOWLING AND FIELDING

	Runs	Wickets	Avg	5 W/I	10 W/M	BB	Ct	St
Test	0	0	0	0	0	—	3	0
First class	16	0	0	0	0	—	209	0

PATSY HENDREN

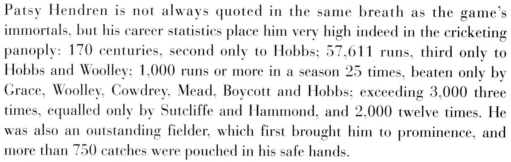

Marcus Williams

Patsy Hendren is not always quoted in the same breath as the game's immortals, but his career statistics place him very high indeed in the cricketing panoply: 170 centuries, second only to Hobbs; 57,611 runs, third only to Hobbs and Woolley; 1,000 runs or more in a season 25 times, beaten only by Grace, Woolley, Cowdrey, Mead, Boycott and Hobbs; exceeding 3,000 three times, equalled only by Sutcliffe and Hammond, and 2,000 twelve times. He was also an outstanding fielder, which first brought him to prominence, and more than 750 catches were pouched in his safe hands.

Figures alone, however, tell little of the man. The universal image of Patsy — it is hard to imagine anyone calling him by his given names, Elias Henry — is of a perky, genial character, an entertainer who loved to play cricket and was as much a favourite of the Lord's crowd in the inter-war years as Compton and Edrich were to be afterwards. The tremendous ovation he received in his final match there, against Surrey in 1937 when he fittingly made a hundred, was proof. He was popular too with his fellow players and would have the dressing-room in uproar with his mimicry and wit.

Hendren in 1930, shortly after his four double centuries and two centuries on the tour to West Indies.

Born of Irish extraction at Turnham Green, near Chiswick, in 1889, Hendren, like many, graduated to Middlesex via the Lord's ground staff. He prided himself that he was never coached and modelled his play on the Lancastrian, Johnny Tyldesley, another compact figure who excelled in the speed of his footwork. Square and muscular, Hendren crouched slightly at the wicket, which made him appear smaller than he actually was. As with all the great batsmen, he possessed a sound and orthodox defence, but his strength and ability made him a master of all the strokes except the late cut. He excelled in the hook and square drive, and late in his career developed a lofted drive to mid-wicket. Above all, he was never dull to watch.

Hendren made his debut for Middlesex (though *Wisden* and the county's history credit the appearance to his brother, Denis) in the infamous 1907 match in which A. C. MacLaren, the Lancashire captain, refused to go on beyond the second day because he claimed the pitch had been deliberately damaged by spectators. Hendren's early years in the side were not blessed with great success and though he was awarded his cap in 1909 after scoring 71

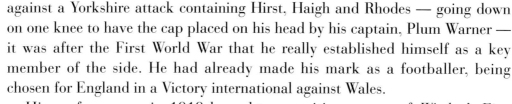

against a Yorkshire attack containing Hirst, Haigh and Rhodes — going down on one knee to have the cap placed on his head by his captain, Plum Warner — it was after the First World War that he really established himself as a key member of the side. He had already made his mark as a footballer, being chosen for England in a Victory international against Wales.

His performances in 1919 brought recognition as one of *Wisden*'s Five Cricketers of the Year and, after heading the national averages in Middlesex's championship-winning summer of 1920, he was selected for the winter tour of Australia. Though he was, by some distance, leading run-maker in all matches, he performed only moderately in the Tests, all of which England lost. He was to go twice more to Australia, each time enjoying greater success outside the Test matches, although on his last visit, in 1928-29, he made a superb 169 in the opening match of the rubber at Brisbane, showing great composure at a crucial stage and then unfolding a fine array of strokes to set England on the way to victory by 675 runs and a 4-1 win in the series.

Hendren enjoyed other successes overseas, not least the 1929-30 tour to the West Indies, when, passing his forty-first birthday, he revelled in the hard pitches to the extent of four unbeaten double centuries — including 205 in the second Test at Port of Spain — and two centuries, and altogether scored 1,765 runs at an average of 135.76. The achievements were all the more meritorious in that, in several of the matches, he faced Constantine bowling at his fastest with a bodyline field. The memories were not lost on Hendren, for, when he faced Constantine and Martindale at Lord's in 1933, he wore a protective cap designed by his wife. It had three peaks, the extra two covering his ears and temples, and was lined with sponge rubber.

Though Hendren's record in home Tests was inconsistent, it had its highlights. He hit successive hundreds against South Africa in 1924 and then 127 not out against Australia at Lord's in 1926, interestingly the only Test century by a Middlesex batsman on his home ground against Australia and one which gave him, a former scorecard seller, the utmost pride. When recalled to the colours against Australia eight years later he helped England to avoid the follow-on with 79 at Trent Bridge and then scored 132 at Old Trafford in the penultimate of his 51 Tests.

For almost two decades he scored prodigiously for Middlesex, frequently

Another mighty blow from Hendren, this time into the top tier of the pavilion at Lord's against Warwickshire in 1920.

PATSY HENDREN

heading the averages, run aggregates and total of centuries, and forming a famous middle-order partnership with his friend, J. W. Hearne. Hendren retired from county cricket in 1937 and went on to coach at Harrow School (his second year in charge saw the first win over Eton for 31 years), Lord's and Sussex and was Middlesex scorer from 1952 to 1960. He died in 1962. Sir Neville Cardus, writing earlier in the year, provided an appropriate epitaph: "His smile, on the field, as well as off it, is so wide that I often expected he would one day be given out 'Smile before wicket'."

E. H. HENDREN MIDDLESEX
BORN 5.2.1889, TURNHAM GREEN, MIDDLESEX

BATTING

	Matches	Innings	Not out	Runs	High score	Avg	100
Test	51	83	9	3,525	205*	47.63	7
First class	833	1,300	166	57,611	301*	50.80	170

BOWLING AND FIELDING

	Runs	Wickets	Avg	5 W/I	10 W/M	BB	Ct	St
Test	31	1	31.00	0	0	1/27	33	0
First class	2,574	48	53.62	1	0	5/43	754	0

cricket heroes

GEORGE HIRST

David Hopps

If county cricket is blessed with a great protector, he must surely be cast in the image of George Herbert Hirst. Lord Hawke, Yorkshire's autocrat, praised Hirst as the greatest county cricketer he knew; Sir Leonard Hutton described him as the most lovable; Bill Bowes suggested he would never meet a better coach — or better man. Yorkshiremen in the early 1900s loved to boast that the world's best all-rounder came from Kirkheaton, batted right-handed and bowled left. Whether the rightful claimant was Hirst or Wilfred Rhodes was a matter for self-indulgent debate. If Rhodes's superior Test record is persuasive, Hirst's brilliance is most apparent in his colossal contribution to county cricket's good fellowship. By the time he stood on the pavilion balcony at the 1921 Scarborough Festival to announce his retirement, 'George Herbert' was 50 years old.

Hirst did the double 14 times — only Rhodes, from the same stone-built village near Huddersfield, dug into the slopes of the Pennines, can surpass that. His double-double in 1906 (more than 2,000 runs and 200 wickets) is unparalleled in its enormity. Hirst's homely retirement speech captured the gentle spirit of a man whose smile, Lord Hawke tells us, "went right round his head and met at the back."

"If I've had any broad views on what they call the game of life, I've learned them on the cricket field," Hirst said. "What can you have better than a nice green field, with the wickets set up, and to go out and do the best for your side? I leave first-class cricket to those who have got to come. I hope they'll have the pleasure in it that I have had."

The father of inswing bowling, Hirst's 'swerve' was almost as revolutionary a force as cricket embarked upon a new century as Bosanquet's unravelling of the googly a few years later. It provided the stocky, broad-shouldered Yorkshireman with a stature well above his 5ft 6ins. He preferred to bowl into a half-headwind, as a left-arm bowler, breezing in from third man, and was particularly deadly when the ball was new or there was moisture about. To this attribute he added a slower ball, a finger-spinner, but the virtues of spin and swerve always bowed to his oft-stated imperative: "Length first." Vital advice from someone troubled by a recurring leg strain for vast portions of his career.

cricket heroes

114

GEORGE HIRST

Hirst's batsmanship was not of the classical vein. It was vigorous, bold and blunt, packed with what the poet William Kerr referred to as "brave Chaucerian pulls." From an unorthodox two-eyed stance, his hearty pull shot, occasionally hauled through square leg off one knee, was as characteristic as Ranji's leg glance.

Such a wholehearted cricketer could have been forgiven a rest in the deep. But when *Wisden*, in 1901, complained of fielders resembling "little mounds of earth" Hirst was held to be an exception. Straight driving was then the fashion and mid-off was nowhere to hide. D. L. A. Jephson wrote: "You may as well drive through a brick wall as pass those iron hands."

George Hirst as portrayed on a postcard at the end of the last century.

Hirst's schooling ended when he was 10 years old. *Vanity Fair* was to remark in 1903: "If he is not a great linguist, he is at least a complete master of the West Riding dialect." He worked as a wirer for a hand-loom weaver, then at a local dye works before his first Yorkshire trial at the age of 18. Hirst recalled: "I wore a sixpenny belt with a snake-clasp and brown boots. My shirt was blue but I got a white one with my first money."

His Yorkshire debut, under Lord Hawke's all-encompassing rule, duly arrived in 1893. England's call followed six years later at Nottingham, W. G.'s farewell Test. By then his brisk, straight left-arm had gained in stealth; as a batsman, who began at No. 10, he had proved Grace's early observation that, "the fellow can bat a bit as well." Throughout his career his doughtiest displays came in the hour of greatest need. Lancashire learned to rue him. In Hirst's eyes, "When you're a batter and a bowler, you're twice as happy," and his first double, in 1896, began to quieten those sages who felt his all-round involvement would become an impossible burden.

The following season, he was involved in one of Yorkshire cricket's most comic interludes, an affair which had lasting repercussions for his own career. Bobby Peel, Yorkshire's left-arm spinner, had a fondness for the bottle. Late at night his drunkenness was a passing embarrassment, but on the morning of a match it was liable to incur Hawke's wrath. Hirst good-naturedly put Peel to bed, before informing his Lordship that he had become "a little queer in the night." His exertions proved in vain as Peel took to the field much the worse for wear. Peel never played for Yorkshire again. Rhodes replaced him and a partnership was forged which was to last beyond the First World War.

c r i c k e t   h e r o e s

GEORGE HIRST

Hirst's record in 24 Tests, 21 against Australia, was sound enough — 790 runs at an average of 22, 59 wickets at 30 apiece. A first tour under A. E. Stoddart in 1897-98 was followed with a place in Pelham Warner's party six years later, yet he did not relish the hot, sleepless nights and the unyielding pitches. Astonished to find a Melbourne 'sticky' during his second visit, Hirst's response spoke of his long-suffering. "When I was in Australia before, I only saw one wet wicket, and that was hung up to dry," he remarked.

If he possessed feelings of failure, they were banished during one remarkable week in 1902 as he was the scourge of the Australian tourists, twice dismissed for less than 40. In the first Test Australia fell in poor light for 36, of which Victor Trumper made half. Hirst's return of 11-4-15-3 was overshadowed by Rhodes's 7-17 but as sound a judge as C. B. Fry opined that there was no clearer case of a bowler taking wickets because of his partner's labours.

Rain rescued the Australians and, somewhat shaken, they journeyed to Headingley where they faced Yorkshire on a treacherous surface which today would attract howls of protest. There is reason to surmise that being Headingley the ball swung lavishly. In the second innings Hirst (7-4-9-5) and F. S. Jackson (7-1-12-5) bundled out the tourists for 23. Hirst described the ball that bowled Trumper as the best of his life.

Hirst's apocryphal grunt to Rhodes — "We'll get 'em in singles" — as England's last pair saved the follow-on against Australia at The Oval later that summer was a tale relished by at least one of Kirkheaton's finest. Rhodes regarded it as flippant. Seven years on came another Ashes confrontation. On a rain-affected Edgbaston pitch, Hirst (9-86 in the match) joined forces with Colin Blythe (11-102) to inspire England's only success.

The century had turned before Hirst gave clue to his greatness. He matured gradually, perhaps urged ahead by Rhodes's mounting reputation. His new-fangled weapon of swerve led Sammy Woods, of Somerset, to wonder: "How the devil can you play a ball that comes in at you like a hard throw-in from cover-point?" Hawke wondered in 1901 if anyone had ever swerved a ball more. Astonishing, then, that Somerset beat Yorkshire that season by 279 runs and left Hirst to brood on figures of 1-189.

Achievements piled high. Hirst's 341 against Leicestershire in 1905 remains Yorkshire's highest individual score. Spared the enthusiasm of a young

cricket heroes

GEORGE HIRST

Hirst was variously described as: the greatest county cricketer of his era, the most lovable, the best coach and the world's best all-rounder.

GEORGE HIRST

substitute fielder, Tom Jayes, he felt he would have reached 400. But for sheer wholeheartedness, the triumph of 1906 remains unsurpassed: 2,385 runs at 45.86; 208 wickets at 6.50. He rubbed his legs with oils to prevent them seizing up; he often bowled with a bandaged knee. Asked if anyone would ever repeat the feat, he replied: "I don't know, but whoever does will be very tired." The crowning glory against Somerset at Bath (111 and 117 not out; 6-70 and 5-45) remains county cricket's greatest individual performance.

Hirst's powers diminished imperceptibly. Indeed, the advent of a Roses match proved an elixir of youth. His 9-23 against Lancashire at Leeds in 1910 was judged the feat of the season. A year later at Old Trafford he followed six wickets with 156. From the last uninterrupted season before the Great War, he salvaged his final double. In 1914 he still had time to bowl Jack Hobbs after a magnificent century at Park Avenue. Hobbs's final six, moments earlier, had knocked back the hour hand of the pavilion clock. "You should have knocked it on to six-thirty, Jack, then we'd have been rid of you," complained the unfortunate bowler, Alonso Drake.

Time *was* rushing on for Hirst but, extraordinarily, war did not force his retirement. Approaching his 48th birthday, he dominated Yorkshire's first post-war match against the MCC at Lord's with an undefeated 180. For many spectators, barely back from the Services, it was perfect therapy.

Long after his retirement, at 58, Hirst bowed once more to the charms of the Scarborough Festival. He made a single, then was bowled by Bowes. The response was typically gracious. "A grand ball that, lad," he said, "I couldn't have played that when I was good."

G. H. HIRST YORKSHIRE
BORN 7.9.1871, KIRKHEATON, YORKSHIRE

BATTING

	Matches	Innings	Not out	Runs	High score	Avg	100
Test	24	38	3	790	85	22.57	0
First class	825	1,215	151	36,323	341	34.13	60

BOWLING AND FIELDING

	Runs	Wickets	Avg	5 W/I	10 W/M	BB	Ct	St
Test	1,770	59	30.00	3	0	5/48	18	0
First class	51,282	2,739	18.72	184	40	9/23	607	0

JACK HOBBS

E. W. Swanton

MR JACK HOBBS.

A 1926 illustration of England's first cricketing knight.

If to be master of one's craft and to wear one's success with modesty and humour is the beau ideal of a sportsman then Jack Hobbs filled his role to perfection. He did so, moreover, over a remarkably long span. Frank Woolley used to say that only those who had seen Jack bat before the war (the first one, of course) could bear witness to the complete, uninhibited stroke-play of those early days — and the young pair played in 19 Tests together pre-war, starting in 1909.

It was just quarter of a century later when in George Duckworth's benefit match at Old Trafford Jack made his 197th hundred. (Pat Hendren with 170 hundreds is next on the list.) A month or two later he bowed quietly out of the Surrey XI. He was coming up to his 52nd birthday, and the legs that had carried him to more runs than anyone had ever made — 61,237 of them — had begun to protest too much for his comfort.

Three men, I would suggest, each in his generation have stood unrivalled in the art of batsmanship, and it seems curiously fitting that their careers should have touched one another. W. G. Grace, who in performance and personality alike had towered over the cricket scene for the best part of forty years, took the field at the Oval for the Gentlemen of England on a chilly spring day of 1905 and saw the Surrey colt Hobbs (J. B.) open the innings and make 88 in just two hours. It was Jack's first first-class match and one of W. G.'s last. The overlapping of Hobbs and Bradman was more protracted, beginning in the 1928/9 Test series in Australia and culminating in Jack's last Test Match, at the Oval in 1930. The Don retired in 1948. Thus it could be said that the genius and influence of the immortal trio pervaded the batting art for three-quarters of a century.

Jack was born at Cambridge on December 16, 1882, son of the Jesus College groundsman and played his first cricket on that sublime stretch all but in the middle of the town known as Parker's Piece. There he came under the influence of the great Tom Hayward.

It is a matter of history that Jack first applied for a trial to the adjacent county of Essex, who simply were not interested. If they had been, who can tell how long it would have been before his inherent quality took him to the top?

c r i c k e t   h e r o e s

JACK HOBBS

Hobbs, left, and Herbert Sutcliffe: regarded as England's finest opening partnership.

What is sure is that Hayward's recommendation to Surrey in 1903 gave him the ideal start. Within two years he was going in first with his mentor on Sam Apted's perfect pitches. Fate saw to it that after the Gentlemen Surrey's first opponents were Essex, who had spurned him. Jack made 155, and Lord Dalmeny (soon to become the Earl of Rosebery) forthwith gave him his cap, one of the swiftest awards ever.

Fortified by such an expression of confidence, he made 1,317 in that first summer, and did even better in his second. In his third he played for the first of 49 times for the Players and was chosen for the MCC 1907/8 tour to Australia. He was already rated the third best professional batsman after Hayward and J. T. Tyldesley. Naturally Jack took advantage of the constant example at the other end of the man "on whose superb example," said *Wisden*, "his own style of batting has obviously been modelled."

Although in the more formalised cricket of Jack's earlier days the attack was generally aimed at or outside off-stump, the Surrey pair were adept at exploiting the leg-side strokes. Jack's repertoire was, however, complete and remained so when in his later years he opened his stance somewhat, the better to cope with the greater prevalence of in-swing. He was of average height and physique, his power deriving from instinctive footwork and perfect timing. He regarded balance and the positioning of the feet as the keys to batting. His advice was always: "Keep it simple."

Whether England and Surrey were doing well or ill there was an extraordinary consistency about his performance. Over his career in England he averaged 0.07 below 50; in Australia it was 51, on the South African mat 68. Yet no-one gave away his wicket more frequently when it mattered little; often enough he reckoned that 100 was sufficient. He had 15 Test hundreds, and on his fifth and last tour of Australia, as senior professional to A. P. F. Chapman, aged 47, said goodbye at Melbourne with two superb innings of 142 and 65. His overall Test average was 56. He was lucky with his opening partners, but how much luckier were those younger men, Sandham and Sutcliffe, in his presence at the other end! Hayward and he reached 100 together 40 times; with Sandham it was 66 times, with Sutcliffe 26. In all, his tally of such partnerships was an unbeatable 166.

He was a marvellous judge of a run, and despite all the thousands of singles

JACK HOBBS

that he and Sutcliffe stole together he was run out only once — from a direct throw by Bradman, following Sutcliffe's call! The number of run-outs he himself achieved was legion. He was the best cover-point of his day, moving around at times apparently uninterested until someone took a liberty. Then came the swoop, the flick and another victim saw his error too late.

Jack was a practising Christian all his life, a fact of which I was reminded not long ago by a reader who remembered how on Sunday mornings his parents used to take their family to church by a longer route from their Streatham home for the pleasure of seeing the Hobbses similarly on their way. This was the sort of veneration which Jack and other household names of his day merited and received. He enjoyed a glass of wine and a cigar, and in congenial company was excellent value. I admired him enormously, but must declare an interest. Leaving Lord's once during a Test at tea-time he explained his going to John Warr: "I've had a good day and seen all my friends, and I can read Jim Swanton in the morning." No compliment ever pleased me more.

J. B. HOBBS SURREY
BORN 16.12.1882, CAMBRIDGE

BATTING

	Matches	Innings	Not out	Runs	High score	Avg	100
Test	61	102	7	5,410	211	56.94	15
First class	825	1,315	106	61,237	316*	50.65	197

BOWLING AND FIELDING

	Runs	Wickets	Avg	5 W/I	10 W/M	BB	Ct	St
Test	165	1	165.00	0	0	1/19	17	0
First class	2,666	107	24.91	3	0	7/56	334	0

Hobbs: a master of the cricketing craft.

LEN HUTTON

Marcus Williams

If he had achieved nothing else in cricket, Len Hutton assured his immortality in the game with one innings at the Oval in 1938. That it was a monumental feat of concentration, lasting for 13 hours 20 minutes, was a matter of awe. That it produced the highest innings hitherto in Test cricket, 364, seized the attention and admiration of the nation. That he eclipsed a record previously held by Don Bradman (334 at Leeds in 1930, an innings which Hutton himself had watched as a spellbound schoolboy) added to the aura of the occasion. That Hutton was aged only 22 made him a very youthful living legend. His, career, however, was to be filled with further honours: the first regular professional captain of England, the man who won back the Ashes after a gap of nearly 20 years, the first professional elected to membership of MCC before the end of his playing days, and the second (after Hobbs) to be knighted for services to cricket.

Born at Fulneck, a mile from Pudsey, in 1916, into a keen cricketing family, he had grown up in Yorkshire's hard cricket school. Graduating from Pudsey St Lawrence, a club which had also nurtured John Tunnicliffe and Herbert Sutcliffe, he made his debut for the county at the age of 17. Though run out for a duck in his first innings, he gave early signs of his prodigious powers of concentration when he scored 196, first in and last out, at Worcester in that same season and was marked down as one with a bright future. The talent, housed in a frame that was never robust, took a while to blossom. The summer of 1937 marked his transition to international ranks, and experience gained from opening the Yorkshire innings with Sutcliffe can have done him no harm. Ten centuries that year included one in his second Test against New Zealand (his first appearance for England had brought only 0 and 1), but his batting was on occasions criticised for its caution. It was, however, acknowledged that he possessed a full and attractive range of strokes, notably the cover drive.

Len Hutton at the Oval in 1938, on his way to 364, and overtaking Bradman's record of 334 set in 1930.

c r i c k e t   h e r o e s

LEN HUTTON

Hutton had presaged his historic innings at the Oval by scoring a century in his first match against Australia, at Trent Bridge in 1938. The 364, through the intervals of which he was nursed by his Yorkshire senior Hedley Verity — a fresh shirt and a cup of tea or a sandwich in the breaks and a visit to the seaside, including some beach cricket, on the Sunday — subjected an essentially shy and retiring man to misgivings about sudden fame and its attendant pressures: his subsequent achievements, buoyed up by a twinkling sense of humour and a steely determination, helped him to cope with the burdens, Hutton suffered a grievous physical blow during the war: in 1941, while serving as an army PT instructor, he fractured his left arm when a mat slipped. After two bone-grafts and eighteen months in hospital he was left with that arm two inches shorter than the right. It was a tribute to his supreme skill that, though he suffered discomfort in the wrist and in his legs from which the bone had been grafted and he had to remodel his technique, his ability remained of the highest class. He was a master batsman in the classical mould, equally formidable on good and bad pitches.

After the war began an opening partnership with the Lancastrian, Cyril Washbrook, that was to serve England well for five years. They were never more successful than in the fourth Test against Australia in 1948, when they put on 168 in the first innings and 129 in the second. This followed the only occasion Hutton was dropped by England after two low scores at Lord's. Until the end of his Test career in 1955 he did not miss another match for which he was available, by when he had scored 6,971 runs (average 56.67) in 79 Tests, including 19 hundreds — figures to rival the best.

He was elevated to the captaincy of England (though he never led or had the ambition to lead his county) against India in 1952 and, directing his troops shrewdly but unobtrusively, he had an outstanding record: 13 wins, six draws and only four defeats. He began with three wins against India and followed with the recapture of the Ashes in 1953 amid unforgettable scenes. Although it was also at the Oval, in 1951, that Hutton achieved the dubious distinction of being the only man to be given out obstructing the field in Tests, it was a favourite ground of his — apart from the 364 he scored three other Test centuries there, two of them doubles, and his hundredth first-class hundred. Little wonder perhaps that it was Surrey he chose as his home when he moved

Hutton at the Oval in 1938: a youthful living legend.

LEN HUTTON

south after his retirement from cricket — though in all other respects he remained Yorkshire through and through.

The other peak of Hutton's captaincy was the 1954-55 series in Australia, when England, with Tyson as spearhead, overwhelmed Australia after losing the first Test. Hutton returned, looking forward with relish to future challenges, but the back trouble, which had begun during the South African tour of 1938-39, was producing unendurable pain. He played his last match for Yorkshire in July 1955; the knighthood in the Queen's birthday Honours the following summer was a fitting tribute to a glorious career. In the years ahead he would make perceptive comments on the game in several newspapers, as well as serving as a Test selector in 1975-77, but, a devoted family man, he would take as much pride in his son Richard's achievements for Cambridge, Yorkshire and England, as he did in his own.

L. HUTTON YORKSHIRE
BORN 23.6.1916, FULNECK, PUDSEY, YORKSHIRE

BATTING

	Matches	Innings	Not out	Runs	High score	Avg	100
Test	79	138	15	6,971	364	56.67	19
First class	513	814	91	40,140	364	55.51	129

BOWLING AND FIELDING

	Runs	Wickets	Avg	5 W/I	10 W/M	BB	Ct	St
Test	232	3	77.33	0	0	1/2	57	0
First class	5,106	173	29.51	4	1	6/76	400	0

RAY ILLINGWORTH

Don Mosey

Raymond Illingworth was the ultimate professional's professional and today, a dozen years after retirement as a player, possesses arguably the shrewdest cricket brain in the world. During the 1989 series of Tests between England and Australia he was commentating at Edgbaston while two of the current England team were sitting in front of a TV set in the dressing-room annexe. Illingworth was explaining to viewers the strategy behind the way Alderman was bowling to Tavare and the two modern practitioners looked at each other, shrugged their shoulders uncomprehendingly and sneered. Two balls later Tavare was out — exactly as Raymond had predicted.

Like his friend and contemporary in the Yorkshire side of the fifties and sixties, Brian Close, Illingworth was a product of the Bradford League and from 1963 to 1968 he was the trusted lieutenant to Close on the field. Where Close had the flair and the instinctive touch of genius, Illingworth supplied the deep thought and analytical mind. Like Close, too, he was a genuine all-rounder who completed the double in six seasons between 1957 and 1964. His greatest success as a Test cricketer came after his departure from Yorkshire to skipper Leicestershire in 1969 and when he became the England captain in that same year. Previously he had earned his place as an off-spinner who might contribute a few runs in the lower order (an understandable selectorial view with a batting order which included Boycott, Edrich, Sharpe, Denness, Fletcher, D'Oliveira and Knight). Now his batting developed both at home and abroad but it was as a tough, uncompromising captain that he made his greatest impact, winning the Ashes in Australia in 1970-71. His philosophy was entirely simple: he demanded 100 per cent fitness for duty from all his players going into a match and total commitment from every one of them while the game was in progress. He asked for nothing more than that from his less gifted players but would tolerate nothing less from the most hugely-talented.

Illingworth's move from Yorkshire to Leicestershire saddened him and excited him simultaneously — saddened because he was (and has remained) a typical Yorkshireman in his grim determination never to be bested if he could avoid it, excited because it presented a new challenge and an opportunity to put his own ideas into practice.

cricket heroes

128

RAY ILLINGWORTH

He arrived at Grace Road to find a team conditioned by years of non-success (Leicestershire had never won a competition of any kind) and, together with the secretary-manager Mike Turner, formed a partnership which saw the county win the Benson & Hedges Cup in 1972 (beating Yorkshire in the final!), the John Player League in 1974, the County Championship and the Benson & Hedges in 1975 and the John Player League again in 1977. Once again he applied a severely practical approach: players must be fit, they must give everything to the team effort.

Raymond started life as a medium-pace seam bowler and a better-than-average batsman, and in a Yorkshire team of the 1950s rich in individual ability but poor in team-effort he quietly learned many lessons. His logical mind told him that Bob Appleyard's ill-health must eventually leave a vacancy for an off-spin bowler and he unobtrusively set about learning a new trade. When Appleyard was finally forced to call it a day in 1958, Yorkshire had a ready-made replacement who could also bat well at No. 5 or 6 and was becoming an accomplished close-to-the-wicket fieldsman. The loss of Johnny Wardle the following year found Illingworth ready to step into his position as a specialist gulley. Raymond was ever a pragmatist.

Though he was not a prodigious spinner of the ball in the Laker mould, Raymond applied the principles of analysis of the opposition and the conditions with painstaking care. He was probably at his best when the wicket was 'dusting' on the third day of county matches but at all times he was concerned to make batsmen work for their runs. He regarded a maiden over bowled by him as a minor triumph and there would be scarcely a delivery in it which had not to be played with care. As a batsman he favoured the on side of the field but he could hit straight and, once he had made up his mind that length and/or line permitted him any liberty, he hit hard.

But it was as a cricket thinker that Illingworth is most respectfully remembered. By the sixties, he knew every experienced player in the game inside out and every new arrival — especially those with any sort of reputation, perhaps from the universities — was studied with clinical care. He had to have a weakness and Raymond would be looking for it. *He* had had to work hard for his own county place and so no-one would have it easy from him.

Similarly, to win an England cap he had to compete with men like Laker,

A genuine all-rounder, Illingworth completed the double of 1,000 runs and 100 wickets on no fewer than six occasions between 1957 and 1964.

RAY ILLINGWORTH

Titmus of Middlesex, Tattersall of Lancashire, Horton of Worcestershire and the Gloucestershire pair, Allen and Mortimore. Until he became captain he was never able to feel that he was firmly established as England's off-spinner. Throughout his entire career 'Illy' could never afford to relax. It is not difficult to see, therefore, why he had no time for those who might have more natural ability but infinitely less application.

He had a turbulent time when he returned to Yorkshire as cricket manager in 1979 and found himself immediately involved in the county's revolution headed by Geoffrey Boycott and his followers. He was appalled by the self-interest of the protagonists. Later he became a radio and TV commentator of admirable quality. The pedantic and pompous might not like his accent or, occasionally, his syntax, but no one outside the England dressing-room could fault his logic or (rarely unkind or ungenerous) appraisal of modern players.

Illingworth, who has never had any time at any stage of his life for the shyster or the poseur, was outstandingly the prime candidate when clamour grew in the mid-eighties for the appointment of a 'supremo' to select and manage the Test team. The job was offered to him in a letter from the TCCB — in terms that he found unacceptable. It was clear that a strong and uncompromising character was not what Lord's wanted, even if the rest of the country did.

Illingworth at the Oval in 1968, after it was announced that he would be leaving Yorkshire following their refusal to offer him a three- or four-year contract.

R. ILLINGWORTH YORKSHIRE AND LEICESTERSHIRE
BORN 8.6.32, PUDSEY, YORKSHIRE

BATTING

	Matches	Innings	Not out	Runs	High score	Avg	100
Test	61	90	11	1,836	113	23.24	2
First class	787	1,073	213	24,134	162	28.06	22

BOWLING AND FIELDING

	Runs	Wickets	Avg	5 W/I	10 W/M	BB	Ct	St
Test	3,807	122	31.20	3	0	6/29	45	0
First class	42,023	2,072	20.28	104	11	9/42	446	0

DOUGLAS JARDINE

Tony Pawson

The first book the Cricket Writers Club produced in 1958 was entitled *Cricket Heroes*. In the introduction Ian Peebles wrote: "Every man should have his heroes. But the very man who shines in the eyes of one may be poison and anathema to another, though in the world of cricket, with which we are concerned, this is unlikely." That last sentence did not hold good when there was a repeat production 25 years later and I was one of the twenty contributors. For I took as my hero the most reviled man in cricket history, Douglas Robert Jardine — for whose courage, determination, and tactical astuteness I have an unbounded admiration. But cricket mythology concocted by men of lesser principle and conviction has portrayed him as a villain, the man who deserved to lose a Dominion rather than win a Test series in Australia by the use of fast leg-theory. What a hard life the English cricket authorities give their captains, with David Gower pilloried and disowned for losing four Tests, Jardine for winning them!

The 'bodyline' series was central to Jardine's cricket career and the quality of the man has to be judged from that momentous tour and the subsequent visit of the West Indies to England. But how had his earlier cricket experience shaped him for so big a responsibility, so controversial a role? Born on 23rd October 1900 he was playing against future Test cricketers at an early age. His preparatory school was Horris Hill near Newbury and their records show him as bowled for a duck by a certain G. O. Allen playing for Summerfields. His main formative years were at Winchester College, where his batting ability and his personality ensured he captained the side.

Gerry Dicker, the keeper of the Wykehamist records, played with him there and recalls him as mature and determined even in his school days: "He was never young. He had a confidence and self-sufficiency beyond his years. As captain of Lords (the Winchester XI) he went his own way and argued down such eminent cricket masters as Harry Altham and Rockley Wilson." That independence of spirit, that courage to take decisions and follow them through made him a fine leader, so there was victory over Eton in 1919 as a culmination of his year as captain, in which his batting skills were clear enough and at that stage his bowling was also a useful asset.

DOUGLAS JARDINE

At Oxford, Jardine was not always at his best, hampered by injury and an addiction to work which was characteristic of his determination to succeed at whatever he undertook, rather than an indication of academic interest. He made little contribution as Oxford lost the 1921 Varsity match by an innings. He did however score two centuries that season and averaged 46.25 in all matches for Oxford, as well as scoring over 1,000 runs and playing for Surrey in the vacation.

Jardine was the leading batsman of 1927 with an average of 91.

With Surrey, Jardine's batting steadily developed. He had a long reach, stood ramrod straight and played with text-book correctness. Combined with his formidable concentration this made him the leading first-class batsman in 1927 with an outstanding average of 91. He was an ideal man to go in anywhere in the first four since he was a fine player of fast bowling, able to score rapidly at need, but by inclination a long innings anchor man. Batting of that quality won him a Test place against West Indies the following year. In his two matches he averaged 52.50 with a top score of 83 run out as contribution to an innings victory. Success against the West Indies, who had yet to become a major force, was followed by selection for all five Tests in the winter tour of Australia. His determined batting there contributed to victory in the first four and a decisive Ashes win.

In that series he played a minor role compared to Hammond, but how useful he was became apparent when their massive partnership set up a narrow victory in the fourth Test. England was struggling after losing two quick second innings wickets when Jardine and Hammond added 262, a record third wicket partnership of which his share was 98. How valuable that proved as England won by just 12 runs. That tour established Jardine as a true Test player at a time when England had a wealth of great batsmen. His turn came to captain the Test side after the happy-go-lucky Percy Chapman had lost out to the Australians in general and a rampant Bradman in particular in 1930. Jardine's induction was easy enough, winning a series against New Zealand and a Test against India in 1932 which set him up for the all-important tour of Australia.

Jardine felt the 1930 series had been lost partly because of the cavalier attitude of the charismatic Chapman and partly because of the dominance of Bradman, whose demoralisation of England's attack had climaxed in that 334 at Leeds. So he complied with his instructions to win in Australia by

c r i c k e t   h e r o e s

JIM LAKER

Despite being a prolific wicket-taker in county cricket (100 or more wickets in a season eleven times and four hat-tricks in the space of seven years) and returning a remarkable 14-12-2-8 in the 1950 Test trial, it was not until the final Test of 1951, only his fourth appearance in three years, that he produced a match-winning return for England with ten wickets at the Oval against South Africa. Also on his home ground, two years later, Laker and his famous spinning partner, Tony Lock, shared eleven wickets to play a prominent part in the recovery of the Ashes, fifteen more to beat the 1955 South Africans, ten against the 1956 Australians and sixteen against the 1957 West Indians. It was the alliance with Lock, Loader and Alec Bedser in a formidable attack which was instrumental in Surrey's unparalleled run of seven successive championships from 1952 to 1958. Laker was at his peak at this period, a destroyer on a turning pitch and constantly probing on easy pitches with his accuracy and variations. He was the finest off-spinner of his day and, in the minds of many, of all time. The foundation of his bowling was a perfect high, side-on delivery and to this he added mastery of flight and considerable powers of spin, stretching his fingers so widely across the seam that the index finger suffered terrible wear.

Maddocks is dismissed for two, Laker wins the Test Match and achieves immortality.

Laker's *annus mirabilis* of 1956, happily coinciding with his benefit year, was the only time he played a full five-match Test series at home and his 46 wickets, at an average of 9.60, have only once been surpassed. It has often been remarked that Lock took only one wicket in 69 overs when Laker claimed his nineteen at Old Trafford (a ground where he had previously had only eight wickets in six Tests). Laker's view was that his partner, frustrated by the lack of reward for superb bowling early on and the constant clatter of wickets at the other end, bowled faster and faster, and consequently shorter and shorter, on a pitch which was unexceptionable at the start — England made 459 by the second afternoon — and grew really difficult only as it dried on the final day. At the end of the sensational proceedings Laker indulged in a dozen polite handshakes, slung his sweater over his left

c r i c k e t   h e r o e s

JIM LAKER

shoulder and jogged gently up the pavilion steps, content to take his greatest triumph in the same way, he said, as he accepted the failures.

Laker retired from first-class cricket in 1959 because of the arthritis in his spinning finger and caused a furore with his ghosted autobiography, *Over To Me*, in which he upset the cricket establishment. He was declared *persona non grata* at the Oval and had his honorary membership of MCC suspended, although both decisions were subsequently rescinded and he went on to serve as chairman of Surrey's cricket committee. He also reappeared as a player, briefly with Norton in the Staffordshire League, and then for Essex from 1962 to 1964. Up to the time of his untimely death in 1986 he established himself as an authoritative television commentator, whose low-key style did not often allow his humour to shine through.

Jim Laker, the finest off-spinner of his day.

J. C. LAKER SURREY AND ESSEX
BORN 9.2.22, FRIZINHALL, BRADFORD, YORKSHIRE

BATTING

	Matches	Innings	Not out	Runs	High score	Avg	100
Test	46	63	15	676	63	14.08	0
First class	450	548	108	7,304	113	16.60	2

BOWLING AND FIELDING

	Runs	Wickets	Avg	5 W/I	10 W/M	BB	Ct	St
Test	4,101	193	21.24	9	3	10/53	12	0
First class	35,791	1,944	18.41	127	32	10/53	271	0

cricket heroes

HAROLD LARWOOD

Alan Ross

It is hard to think of a character less suited to the limelight, even less to being the centre of notorious controversy, than Harold Larwood. The main protagonist in 1932/33 of Bodyline, the bowling of fast, short-pitched balls on the line of the body to a legside field, Larwood was never more responsible than the infantryman who is ordered to go over the top. The theory was conceived by others and the orders given by the captain D. R. Jardine. In his previous Test series against England, that of 1930, Bradman had made scores of 8, 131, 254, 1, 334, 14, 232 — an average of 139.14. Larwood in that series had taken 4 for 292, and was dropped for one Test. Australia won the series.

Something needed to be done. Larwood had already played a series in Australia, that of 1928-29, when he took 18 wickets for 728 — including 6 for 32 in the first Test at Brisbane. He bowled then to a conventional fast bowler's field. Bradman averaged 66.85. At the end of the Bodyline series Bradman averaged 56, Larwood had taken 33 wickets at an average of 19.51, and England had won by four Tests to one.

Bodyline, then, could be designated, in practical terms, a success. But the feelings it aroused did great damage to the relationship between England and Australia, and Larwood himself was so upset by the criticism that he declined to play against Australia when they next appeared in England in 1934. Larwood, who had demonstrated such phenomenal speed and accuracy in carrying out instructions, was never again a Test bowler of consequence. He was obliged, as a result of the strain imposed on his left leg, to cut down his run and to bowl at nowhere near his original pace.

Neville Cardus, watching this secondary Larwood bowl in his last season, was moved to write: "Fast bowling is dying out. And Gover runs on the flat of his feet, and bowls not much faster off the pitch than the Larwood of today; Larwood who now is compelled to use the canter of compromise instead of his old lovely gallop over the earth, head down, like a young colt chafing his bit."

Cardus was rather too keen to write off the modern player. "Larwood was the last of the classical bowlers," he wrote, "he showed his left side to the batsman, as Tom Richardson did. His body swung over the right hip, and his

Harold Larwood was a true 'strike' bowler, best used in short, sharp spells.

HAROLD LARWOOD

follow-through was thrilling." But Lindwall, a decade or so later, bowled with the same lovely flowing action, Bedser and Lillee showed their left shoulders to the batsman, and certainly Frank Tyson, in 1954/55, must have been as fast.

Ian Peebles has given the most evocative description of Larwood in action: "He ran about 18 yards, accelerating with controlled rhythmical strides, on the last of which his shoulders opened with a long swing of his fully extended arms. His right hand described a great arc starting from near the calf of his leg, and, at full pressure, his knuckles would touch the pitch on his follow-through. Co-ordination was perfect, so that the whole concerted effort was applied to the moment of delivery."

The last of the classical bowlers? Neville Cardus certainly thought so.

Larwood came from mining stock and mining country. He was rather less than medium height, but in any photograph his head was raised an inch or two by the thick shock of hair cut flat across the top. He was stocky in the manner of Fred Trueman, and he had to contend for far too much of his playing life with unresponsive, doped pitches. In the circumstances it was surprising that he lasted as long as he did, 1924-38, even though the last four seasons were at half-cock.

In Larwood's time, the 1920s and 30s, professional cricketers did not on the whole ask for much and they did not get much. They had, most of them, the manner and speech of countrymen. Larwood may have been exceptional, but only in his bowling. All those who knew him and played with him remarked on his unassuming character, of his domestic nature. "In cricket between the wars," Robertson-Glasgow once wrote, "the two most magnificent sights that I have seen were Hammond batting and Larwood bowling... in both these cricketers I have found something heroic, something of immortal fire, which conquers argument."

The career of Larwood, "who blew like a gale and bent the flower of Australia," Robertson-Glasgow puts as a mere eight years. It was a fact that, even more than most fast bowlers, Larwood had to be nursed. He was in the real sense a 'strike' bowler, best used in short, lethal spells. Despite the long arms and strong back the frame could only stand so much. It is not recorded that Harold Larwood had much to say outside cricket. While the Gods once lifted him to something like immortality they put him down again, gently and soon, when they had no more use for him.

HAROLD LARWOOD

So Larwood by the age of 30 had bowled his last ball in a Test match and returned to the unspectacular circuit of the county grounds. He never lost his Nottinghamshire accent, he took up shopkeeping, and he and his wife produced five daughters. The times in England were not good to him and he made the long voyage to Australia with his family. He settled peacefully in what had once been enemy territory and he spoke sometimes with visiting English cricketers who felt honoured to be able to call on him. He was, after all, the man with whose name fast bowling was synonymous.

H. LARWOOD NOTTINGHAMSHIRE
BORN 14.11.04, NUNCARGATE, NOTTS

BATTING

	Matches	Innings	Not out	Runs	High score	Avg	100
Test	21	28	3	485	98	19.40	0
First class	361	438	72	7,290	102*	19.91	3

BOWLING AND FIELDING

	Runs	Wickets	Avg	5 W/I	10 W/M	BB	Ct	St
Test	2,212	78	28.35	4	1	6/32	15	0
First class	24,994	1,427	17.51	98	20	9/41	234	0

PETER MAY

Jack Bailey

Peter May was a product of the orthodox route to cricket fame as a player in the days when he adorned the first-class game, as an amateur captain of England and later of Surrey. Fast, true wickets at Charterhouse formed an excellent proving ground for his outstanding natural ability. George Geary, the great Leicestershire bowler, then a sympathetic and kindly coach, was there to guide where guidance was necessary. Then there was Fenner's to bat on during his Cambridge University days, those true pitches which lent added confidence to the virtually mature player who wanted to hone and burnish an already formidable technique.

By the time he played for England, first against South Africa in 1951, he was undoubtedly a player with all the trappings of potential greatness. That his quiet demeanour and classical unfussy style was matched by the temperament and determination to succeed was eloquently stated when he made a century in his first Test match appearance at Lord's. He was 21 years of age.

Already his immaculately straight bat and unerring judgement of length were in place, as was the power of his driving off front foot and back on both sides of the wicket. He thrived, especially, on the ball coming into him (much of the bowling fed this particular strength in those days) and mid-on and mid-wicket were often given, as they say, a torrid time of it.

He went on to captain the national team more often than any other Englishman before or since, leading England on 41 occasions, 35 of them in consecutive matches. He was a natural. Playing under Len Hutton immediately before he himself took over the captaincy, he learned from the master's tactical shrewdness as he had also learned from Surrey's Stuart Surridge. Surrounded for the most part by professional bowlers of the highest class and inheriting early on a fast bowling battery which still contained the likes of Tyson, Trueman and Statham, he earned his team's respect as much for the quality of his own batting performances as for the steely resolve contained within a quiet, reserved exterior.

Those of his contemporaries who played against him at the highest level are virtually unanimous in their assessment of him as the greatest English batsman whose career began post-war. For all his orthodoxy he could be impossible to

DEREK RANDALL

specialist batsmen. In came Randall at number three, again forced into too high a position by the selfishness of his colleagues. "You're sacrificing him, man!" shouted a West Indian in the crowd, "You're sacrificing him!"

The man was right. Derek Randall played out his eccentric days with Nottinghamshire and was never chosen for England again.

D. W. RANDALL NOTTINGHAMSHIRE
BORN 24.2.51, RETFORD, NOTTS

BATTING

	Matches	Innings	Not out	Runs	High score	Avg	100
Test	47	79	5	2,470	174	33.37	7
First class	427	726	68	24,740	237	37.59	44

BOWLING AND FIELDING

	Runs	Wickets	Avg	5 W/I	10 W/M	BB	Ct	St
Test	3	0	—	0	0	—	31	0
First class	386	12	32.16	0	0	3/15	315	0

K.S.RANJITSINHJI

Alan Ross

K. S. Ranjitsinhji, His
Highness the Maharajah
Jam Sahib of Nawangar
— 'Ranji'

There are more varied photographs of K. S. Ranjitsinhji — His Highness the Maharajah Jam Sahib of Nawanagar — than of any other famous cricketer. But then Ranji was cricket's most various character, whose life had many parts, which the portraits illustrate. There is, first, Ranji at Cambridge, pale blue cap perched on a roundish, moustached face. Next, Ranji with a tennis racquet, tennis being a game at which he then excelled. F. S. Jackson, the Cambridge cricket captain, was puzzled by this untutored Indian and thought little of him as an undergraduate, his reputation then as much for extravagance as for games-playing. He got his Blue, but had a moderate match at Lord's, despite having engaged — in the grand manner — a series of professional coaches to bowl at him.

Ranji, though he had little money, was not shy of acting the Rajput Prince; soon he was hiring billiard markers, renting fishing rights and shoots. The pictures show him dressed for the part, now with a parrot, Popsey, on one shoulder. Popsey, already over fifty when Ranji acquired her, survived her owner, though bald, blind, and querulous. Other photographs of the time show Ranji at the wheel of his own car, the first ever to be seen in Cambridge. He is seen in fine jewelry, in immaculately tailored suits. Ranji's home State was a poor one, his grant modest. The tailors and others had to wait a long time for payment.

Ranji left Cambridge in 1894, spending that summer qualifying for Sussex, the county where his friend C. B. Fry was already installed. Ranji had played for Cambridge against Sussex at Hove and had taken a liking to the place, its Oriental flavour and Regency raffishness. It was with Sussex in 1895 that Ranji's career really blossomed. In that first season, 1895, Ranji hit four hundreds, two at Hove, two at Lord's. He was suffering from the asthma that was eventually to kill him, but he still finished third in the first-class averages, scoring 1,766 runs at an average of 50.16. Only Grace and MacLaren were above him.

From 1895 to 1904, except for 1898, which season he took off to spend in India on his way home from Australia, Ranji was one of the glories of English cricket. He hit 72 centuries — ten of them in 1896, thirteen in 1900 — mostly

MOONSHINE'S CRICKETERS.—MR. K. S. RANJITSINHJI.

K.S.RANJITSINHJI

Spy's view of Ranji as it appeared in Vanity Fair.

for Sussex, but two of the greatest for England, 154 not out against Australia at Manchester in his first Test match, 175 against Australia at Sydney. In 1899 and 1900 he made over 3,000 runs, in 1900 hitting five double centuries. Statistics are one of the least interesting things about Ranji, but even if he had been one of the more plodding, rather than the most elegant, of players, they would have been telling.

What Ranji did, in his unique fashion, was add new dimensions to the art of batting. He turned defence into attack, substituting the forcing back stroke for the forward push, so that if the ball was well up he drove, if on a length or short he slashed it away past cover. He was a beautiful late cutter and glancer to leg, merely hastening the ball on its way by the finest of deflections. He was exceptionally light on his feet, a savager of spin bowling by his quickness down the pitch.

There is one particularly famous portrait of Ranji's stance, posed at Hove. It is relaxed and at ease, the feet at ten to two, the bat resting gently on the ground at 45 degrees. Hutton 50 years later stood in much the same way. To the same date belong the series of still pictures showing Ranji going through his repertoire: the drive to leg, the square slash, the leg glance, with feet crossed. The earliest group photographs show Ranji in his first season for Sussex, on the right of and dwarfed by the huge figure of W. L. Murdoch. Next, he is himself captain, in 1901, Fry on his left; then, in straw boater, on the *Ormuz*, Australia-bound. Now we come upon Ranji entertaining W. G. Grace, Grace carrying two golf clubs and Ranji smiling in the protection of Grace's enfolding arms. Finally the last of the cricket photographs, Ranji aged 40 at the Oval, 1912, the slim figure replaced by the heavy, middle-aged body of the ruling prince. Cardus once referred to Ranji as the "midsummer's night's dream of cricket" but after 1907, when Ranji was installed as Jam Sahib of Nawanagar, cricket took second place.

We see Ranji next in full regalia aboard an elephant on the way to his installation; Ranji, gun on his shoulder and a cheetah at his feet; Ranji, in army uniform on leave from France; Ranji among his fellow princes at Baroda, head turned sideways to hide his glass eye, the right one lost in a shooting accident. From 1907 on Ranji was less the English cricketer, more the Indian potentate. He was one of India's three representatives at the first assembly of the League

K.S.RANJITSINHJI

of Nations in Geneva, later a highly respected member of the Council of Princes. But for the last 26 years of his life his duties as Jam Sahib of Nawanagar claimed most of his attention. "The prince of a little State but the King of a great game," it was said of Ranji. It was also said of him that it was only in the company of Englishmen that he was ever happy. His loyalty to the country that gave him both fame and serenity was complete; but though he may have left his heart in England it was as a solitary, rather melancholy Indian that he had to live out his life.

K. S. RANJITSINHJI SUSSEX
BORN 10.9.1872, SARODAR, INDIA

BATTING

	Matches	Innings	Not out	Runs	High score	Avg	100
Test	15	26	4	989	175	44.95	2
First class	307	500	62	24,692	285*	56.37	72

BOWLING AND FIELDING

	Runs	Wickets	Avg	5 W/I	10 W/M	BB	Ct	St
Test	39	1	39.00	0	0	1/23	13	0
First class	4,601	133	34.59	4	0	6/53	233	0

WILFRED RHODES

Derek Hodgson

Wilfred Rhodes was 22 when he first played for England in 1898 and entered the last of his 58 Test matches in 1926, when he was 49. He bowled to W. G. Grace and to Bradman, and on those facts alone he would be remembered as one of the greatest cricketers. But his Test matches were only the diamonds in one of the richest seams of talent ever found in Yorkshire and England.

He had, as Peter Thomas pointed out, three separate careers: as a slow left arm bowler of phenomenal accuracy and patience he displaced Johnny Briggs in the England side in his second season; his batting developed so well, particularly his defensive technique, that he became Jack Hobbs's regular partner as England opening batsman in Australia; and after the Great War, when both Yorkshire and England had need for him to bowl again, in the front line, he reverted to bowling — at the age of 33 — with, astonishingly, a third of his career still to run. He was only half way through that career when he was granted his county benefit; by today's reckonings Wilfred Rhodes was entitled to ask Yorkshire for three benefits... and he would have deserved them!

In a first-class career spanning over thirty years Wilfred Rhodes had the unique privilege of bowling to two of cricket's greats, W. G. Grace and Don Bradman.

As a boy, in Kirkheaton near Huddersfield, he grew up in the shadow of George Hirst, six years his senior, although both were to open the bowling for the club. Kirkheaton once dismissed Slaithwaite for 9 — Hirst 5 for 2, Rhodes 5 for 3, the four byes being explained by the scorer: "Ower stumper were reight freetened o' George Herbert." Hirst bowled quick left arm and was famous, Rhodes was another trier a long way behind the reigning left-arm monarch Bobby Peel.

But the boy was determined. He learned to bowl on a patch of grass cut by his father near their cottage. In winter, or in bad weather, he bowled in a woodshed, measuring his spin by coating one side of the ball with chalk. He found employment in the railway engine sheds at Mirfield, finishing at two o'clock on Saturday afternoons, which meant he had to run three miles to Kirkheaton in order to play in a match starting at 2.30.

One Saturday the foreman found the young Rhodes ringing the knocking-off bell at 1.30. He was sacked but, after a spell labouring, got a job as a cricket professional in Galashiels — the source of the story that Rhodes was taught to bowl in the Borders. Like any good 'pro' he had to bowl as circumstances

WILFRED RHODES

dictated — fast, medium or slow — but the experience was valuable and he was waiting to be called up for a trial with Warwickshire when the cricket world was stunned by the news of Peel's sacking.

Even then the door was not opened for Rhodes alone — ahead of him was Albert Cordingley of Bradford. In an end-of-season trial Cordingley took 8 for 33 against the colts and 3 for 62 against the seniors, Rhodes managed only 2 for 99 against the first team. However, both were included in the party for the opening match against MCC at Lord's and tales vary as to why Rhodes won his place ahead of Cordingley — Hawke and F. S. Jackson both asserting afterwards that he was their first choice. History records that Rhodes took 6 for 33 on his debut. He was retained to play against Somerset at Bath while the unlucky Cordingley, before he could be given his chance, was recalled by telegram to attend his mother's funeral. In his absence Rhodes added match figures of 13 for 45 and a titanic career was launched.

Rhodes took 141 wickets in his first season, immediately becoming one of *Wisden*'s five. He played for England in his second season and went on to do the double of 100 wickets and 1,000 runs in a season 16 times. In 29 consecutive summers he was absent from the top twenty of the averages only four times. In his three finest summers he collected 594 victims!

His secret, according to his contemporaries, lay in his absolute command of flight. A ball bowled above the batsman's eyeline, he believed, was more difficult to play because an adjustment had to be made; his opinion on what passes for spin bowling today would be illuminating. As a young man, on the under-prepared and rarely-covered pitches of that time, he could spin the ball wickedly. As preparation improved and he had to adapt to harder pitches abroad he tended to reserve his spin for the right conditions.

Not that batsmen, especially the beginners, were ever sure as to what Wilfred was doing. He would say: "If they think it's spinning, it's spinning." The longer he played, the more information he stored to feed a sagacious brain, and his ability to tease and test a batsman by fractionally varying his length and direction became legend. Cardus thought his greatest performance was in 1903 in Sydney when Australia, on a pitch described as hard and polished, raised 500. Victor Trumper made 185 and it was said of that innings that he had three strokes for every ball. Rhodes finished with figures of 5 for 94 off 48

WILFRED RHODES

overs, many of them bowled at Trumper, who was reported to have called down the wicket after yet another maiden: "Please Wilfred, give me a little peace."

Either side of the Great War Rhodes enjoyed a lordly status — sage, guru, tactician and brilliant performer. A line of Yorkshire captains deferred to him and some of the tales told then are repeated today. A young amateur hit the first two balls he received for four whereupon his partner Rhodes walked down the pitch to remonstrate: "Ay op, lad. We doan't play this gayam for foon." He was never a boastful man, just matter-of-fact when he went into retirement and said: "Ah were niver cut and ah were niver pulled."

He spent his later years with his daughter in Bournemouth, his eyesight failing fast, appearing occasionally at Lord's on the arm of one of his great contemporaries, happy to listen to the sounds of the game, his judgements as shrewd as ever. A taciturn man in his playing days, Cardus met him again when Rhodes was 73 and was surprised to find that the old man, then blind, could not stop talking. A grateful Cardus remembered: "History came from his mouth in rivers."

It was Rhodes who first demolished and yet paradoxically reinforced one of the greatest stories in Test history. In 1902 at the Oval, England, needing 263 to beat Australia, were reduced to 48 for 5. Jessup hit a glorious 104 out of 139 in 74 minutes and 15 were wanted when last man Rhodes joined Hirst, who is supposed to have said to his Kirkheaton junior: "We'll get 'em in singles." Rhodes said afterwards that no words were exchanged. Who needed words? ... they got 'em in singles!

Rhodes poses for the camera in 1927, the year after his final appearance in a Test match.

W. RHODES YORKSHIRE
BORN 29.10.1877, KIRKHEATON, YORKSHIRE

BATTING

	Matches	Innings	Not out	Runs	High score	Avg	100
Test	58	98	21	2,325	179	30.19	2
First class	1,097	1,528	237	39,802	267*	30.83	58

BOWLING AND FIELDING

	Runs	Wickets	Avg	5 W/I	10 W/M	BB	Ct	St
Test	3,425	127	26.96	6	1	8/68	60	0
First class	69,993	4,187	16.71	287	68	9/24	764	0

c r i c k e t   h e r o e s

JOHN SNOW

Doug Ibbotson

"To be great is to be misunderstood." So wrote the American philosopher-poet, Ralph Waldo Emerson. John Augustine Snow, another philosopher-poet and also an outstanding fast bowler, may or may not have have been familiar with the quotation but, during an often controversial 16-year career with Sussex and England, he was certainly well aquainted with the sentiment.

The legacy remains. While such names as Trueman and Statham, Tyson and Willis spring readily into the popular perception, few but those who know and understand Snow, the person, can recall with certainty the exemplary achievements of Snow, the cricketer. One reason for this phenomenon is that Snow was seldom perceived to be of equable disposition either by the contemporary media-man-in-the-street or, more pertinently, by those who directed his talents. The other reason was that Snow's resentment of this misunderstanding simply exacerbated the general impasse and led to further manifestation of disinterest or discontent.

As a consequence he was frequently reprimanded and sometimes dropped — a circumstance which moved him to pen the following lines: "Standing on a still summer's day, eye watching swallows earth-hugging insect-chasing way, wondering what to do, knowing that it always happens and now it's happened to you. What not again? Yes. Feel like laughing at the fable yet not being able because you have no middle and life waits watching behind having given you the casual twiddle. Yet as your world revolved it spun you through a wider sky, opened further open eye, it's a game... "

Here is encapsulated the persona of a man who could say little but divulge a whole segment of his sincerity as opposed to some who said much, ostensibly in friendship, but who, in fact, said nothing. A man who could and did shut out the insincere who sought to invade his esoteric sanctum but who quietly confided all to those of similar mind with whom he might be less acquainted.

Thus, during his playing career, he was variously described as moody, impassive and aloof. One contemporary observed: "It is difficult to know whether there is more in him than meets the eye — or less. On a routine day at Hove nothing in him meets the eye at all. Whereas others can look merely distracted or detached, Snow manages to become non-apparent — a pale,

cricket heroes

JOHN SNOW

ghostly presence going through the motions. His time-clock is one of his own adjustment which bears no relation to the needs of the captain."

Certainly Snow was not readily motivated by the mundane and generally bowled with less enthusiasm for Sussex than England, for whom in 49 Tests he captured 202 wickets at 26.66. Against world-class opposition these figures speak for themselves compared with a career return of 1,174 at 22.72 against all and (often) sundry batsmen.

Though slimly built and little more than medium height he was capable of genuine pace, delivered with a smooth, high and beautifully controlled action. His essential method was to slant the ball into the batsman and cut it sharply off the pitch. By sheer aggression rather than physical attribute he had the ability to extract lift from even the flattest surface and could produce a dangerous bouncer. If there was a flaw it was his tendency to bowl a fairly generous quota of no-balls.

It was consistent with Snow's temperament that some of his better performances for Sussex closely followed his rejection, for one reason or another, by England. For example, after being dropped during the New Zealand tour of 1969, he taunted the selectors by routing Hampshire with a match analysis of 10 for 80. He was doubtless making a particular point, too, when he produced his career-best 8 for 87 against Middlesex — at Lord's.

Perhaps the most infamous incident involving Snow's uncertain temperament occurred at Lord's in 1971 when he body-checked Sunil Gavaskar, who was running between wickets, and spread-eagled the Indian batsman on the pitch. Another disciplinary action. "What, not again? Yes..." But to dwell on such aspects is to fall into the trap that shuts out the best of Snow. Beneath the skin-deep cynicism and detachment lay an elegant personality, warmed by honest beliefs and glowing pride.

When dropped after the first Test against the West Indies in 1967/8 he knew he had bowled badly and gracefully accepted the decision. Recalled for the third Test at Sabina Park, he claimed 7 for 49 and went on to take 27 wickets in the series. It was a performance surpassed only by his magnificent bowling for Illingworth's victorious side in Australia, 1970/71. Throughout that tour, as often before, Snow strode virtually alone at the head of the strike-force, yet emerged from the Test series with 31 wickets, average 22.8.

cricket heroes

JOHN SNOW

In that same series, Snow the batsman also surpassed himself with an average of 23.50 — which was almost ten runs more per innings than he achieved in his overall career. Though it clearly did not apply on this occasion — and again to touch on his underlying commitment — as Snow recognised towards the end of his career that his bowling was marginally on the decline, the more conscientiously he applied himself to his batting which, though not of all-round quality, was undertaken with determination.

Too introspective, perhaps, to become a sporting TV personality, nor yet a best-selling man of literature, Snow initially retired from the public limelight into peripheral business to re-emerge only briefly in the late 80s as a stand-by coach for Sussex — the chiselled features and athletic bearing seemingly untouched by time.

Snow sends down another fierce delivery in the Test match against Australia at Lord's in 1975.

*"So come on, who's king of the castle
now I'm the dirty rascal,
standing, on a still summer's day
eye watching swallows insect-chasing way..."*

J. A. SNOW   SUSSEX
BORN 13.10.41, PEOPLETON, WORCESTERSHIRE

BATTING

	Matches	Innings	Not out	Runs	High score	Avg	100
Test	49	71	14	772	73	13.54	0
First class	346	451	110	4,832	73*	14.17	0

BOWLING AND FIELDING

	Runs	Wickets	Avg	5 W/I	10 W/M	BB	Ct	St
Test	5,387	202	26.66	8	1	7/40	16	0
First class	26,675	1,174	22.72	56	9	8/87	125	0

c r i c k e t   h e r o e s

BRIAN STATHAM

Trevor Bailey

My first encounter with Brian Statham was when he and Roy Tattersall were flown out to Australia as replacements for Doug Wright and myself, who had been injured. Brian's was an intriguing selection, as he had only played in 14 Lancashire matches and had taken a mere 36 wickets. I had my doubts about sending somebody quite so inexperienced, but he had impressed Len Hutton in the Roses match and that should have been enough, because Len was an outstanding judge of players, particularly quick bowlers. In 1951 Brian was a fast medium and not the genuine fast bowler he was to become, indeed at that stage a shade slower than myself. What impressed everyone immediately was his accuracy, which was indeed to become such a feature of his bowling. Unlike most young quickies, Brian's control of line and length was exceptional, and was reflected by his finishing second in the overall bowling averages with his 11 wickets costing 20 runs apiece.

He went on to become the most accurate fast bowler I have played with, or against. He believed in that simple but effective formula which holds that when a batsman fails to make contact the ball will hit the stumps. As a result of an action that was a shade open, but suited Brian, he was a seam, rather than a swing bowler, seldom moving the ball in the air. On the other hand, his right arm was beautifully high at the moment of delivery, and chased his left arm across the body until checked by the left hip in classical fashion. He was double jointed and very supple with a graceful, athletic run up, which combined to give him a whippy delivery that made the ball nip off the pitch rather more quickly than expected. As a result his movement was into the right handed batsman, though he occasionally made one come back off the seam. Indeed, one such ball removed Jeff Stollmeyer's off stump in the Guyana Test after pitching on middle and leg.

Although averages over a short period can be untrustworthy, figures over a career cannot lie and Brian's show him to be truly a great fast bowler. In his 70 Tests, including numerous tours spread over more than a decade, he took 252 wickets at 24.84, while his total haul in his eighteen year first class career was 2,260 wickets at just over 16 apiece, underlining again his control, which also applied to his temperament. Unlike the majority of the pace bowling fraternity

Exceptional control of line and length made Brian Statham a bowler of enormous value to county and country.

BRIAN STATHAM

Statham takes his 250th wicket in Test Matches as 'Tiger' Lance of South Africa is given out lbw.

— who tend to be aggressive, not infrequently abusive, and liable to extravagant anger — Brian was entirely reliable. He never indulged in histrionics, nor provided misbehaviour headlines; he simply went on bowling fast and straight at the stumps irrespective of the conditions, which is why every captain wanted him in his side. Philosophically, he accepted bowling uphill into the wind, dropped catches, bad decisions, and 0 for plenty on a 'featherbed' with rueful smile and an occasional dry aside.

I can count on the fingers of one hand the times I have seen him ruffled. There was that occasion at Melbourne when, after taking 5 for 57, his batting colleagues surrendered and he found himself walking to the crease instead of enjoying a glass of lager and smoking a cigarette with his feet up. He also, understandably, took exception to a batsman walking down the pitch to him and once, after a West Indian batsman had been given not out caught after Fred Trueman had nearly broken his thumb, Brian produced a couple of venomous chest-tickling bouncers when he resumed his innings, which both surprised and hurt him, as Brian used the bumper as a very occasional shock ball. I often felt, that is when he was on my side, he might have employed it rather more frequently.

Endowed with a tough wiry frame and plenty of stamina, Brian was never a training enthusiast. He kept fit by bowling, rather than training in order to be fit to bowl, and he was able to manage long spells without too much strain. His ability to keep going over after over without any perceptible loss of pace or accuracy meant there was a danger of his being over bowled, but fortunately he usually recovered quickly. One occasion when this did not occur was at Lord's against South Africa in 1955 when Peter May called upon him to bowl unchanged throughout the South African second innings. He finished with 7 wickets for 39, with one of the finest examples of sustained fast bowling, which won us the match, but Brian was never really himself again that summer.

Brian was half of two immortal international bowling partnerships — Tyson and Statham and Trueman and Statham. His style of bowling, penetrating and economical, provided the ideal contrast. The unfortunate batsman trying to escape from the fire of Frank, or Fred, found himself having to play almost every ball at the other end, so it would be true to say that the success of both owed much to the tremendous and unselfish support they received from him.

c r i c k e t   h e r o e s

FRANK TYSON

He was not a beautiful bowler and used a very powerful, rather low 'draggers' action which put a great strain on his ankle and body, which is why his career was so relatively short and why he only played in 17 Tests. His pace was derived from broad shoulders, a very strong back and the ability to bring his right arm over very quickly.

Because he gained a degree at Durham University, Frank came into the first class game later than most fast bowlers. Strangely, as exceptional pace is instantly recognisable and very valuable, he was turned down by Lancashire and joined Northants. I first encountered him at Romford in 1954, and though he bowled me out and his speed was alarming, what left the largest impression was his ultra-long, ungainly run up. He was also decidedly erratic, though his pace meant that many of his loose deliveries went unpunished. I was, in fact, surprised when he was selected for Australia, as he had only taken 78 wickets during the summer, whereas Fred Trueman, who had picked up 134 at 15 apiece was not invited, but Len Hutton appreciated the value of pure speed on Australian pitches and in their atmosphere. This was not immediately obvious, as we made the mistake, in the days when the ball did not retain its shine and seam, of going into the first Test at Brisbane with four seam bowlers — Bedser, Statham, Tyson and myself — forgot balance, ignored two high class spinners in Wardle and Appleyard, and invited the opposition to bat first.

Australia answered with 601 for 8 declared, we lost by an innings and plenty and Frank, using his long run, finished with 1 for 160 in 29 overs. However, we had noticed that in the nets Frank appeared to be just as quick and rather more accurate off an abbreviated run up. So, after that first heavy defeat, Frank employed a thirteen pace approach, which not only gave him greater control, but also took much less out of himself. It was not as if he flowed into bowl, like Mike Holding or Wes Hall, so his run-up was less important. The only thing lost was the fascinating spectacle of Frank setting off with the wicketkeeper crouching some seventy to eighty yards away. In his short approach, a somewhat laboured affair, he assumed the appearance of a cross between a Sherman tank and a Welsh front row forward in top gear, somebody to have on your side in a battle, but definitely not to be entrusted with a tray full of drinks in a delicate lounge, as the odds of him either tripping over something, or knocking into somebody were far too high.

cricket heroes

FRANK TYSON

In the last four Tests of the 1954-55 series Frank, using his abbreviated run up, destroyed and demoralised the Australians taking 27 wickets. It was the highlight of his career, and he never achieved comparable success again. There were several reasons. First, Frank did not swing the ball, like Fred Trueman, nor move it off the seam, like Brian Statham; his main weapon was speed. Second, most Northants pitches tended to be slow and favoured spin, and the wicket at Peterborough where he took 5 for 18 against Essex was a rare exception. Third, on a considerable number of English county pitches the accurate seamer, such as Derek Shackleton, was more effective, though less frightening, because he made the ball deviate so much more. Fourth, at the moment of release Frank's action was low, so he achieved less lift than several bowlers who were not so fast, but had higher arm actions. This also applied to his bouncer, which was easier to negotiate than Peter Loader's. Finally, and the most important reason why his haul of wickets in his eight seasons with Northants was only 525 and his appearances for England at home a handful, was recurring injury due to the strain of bowling very fast without the rhythm of a Wes Hall, or a Fred Trueman, and having to depend upon power.

It was always an experience and a challenge, batting against Frank. My tactics were to play straight and try to exploit his pace, rather than attempting to hit the ball, which brought about the downfall of so many talented Australian batsmen. I never considered a cut unless I had been in for more than an hour, as it would have been in Keith Andrew's gloves before I had completed the shot.

A fearsome sight for any batsman as Tyson unleashes the ball at full power.

F. H. TYSON NORTHAMPTONSHIRE
BORN 6.6.30, FARNWORTH, LANCASHIRE

BATTING

	Matches	Innings	Not out	Runs	High score	Avg	100
Test	17	24	3	230	37*	10.95	0
First class	244	316	76	4,103	82	17.09	0

BOWLING AND FIELDING

	Runs	Wickets	Avg	5 W/I	10 W/M	BB	Ct	St
Test	1,411	76	18.56	4	1	7/27	4	0
First class	16,030	767	20.89	34	5	8/60	85	0

cricket heroes

DEREK UNDERWOOD

Doug Ibbotson

When Derek Leslie Underwood finally bequeathed his clinker-built boots to the Thames Lightermen in the autumn of 1987, Kent and England said farewell to a cricketer who, for 24 summers, had confounded the purists and staggered the statisticians by perfecting an unique style of bowling that defied convention, dismayed master-batsmen and enthralled a million spectators who cared not for the esoteric incongruities so long as their expectations were fulfilled. And fulfilled they invariably were.

During a first-class career which began when he was a 17-year-old stripling, Underwood claimed more than 2,450 wickets — 297 of them (average 25.83) in 86 Tests — and would undoubtedly have broken all Test records had he not been penalised for 'defecting' to World Series Cricket and, later, to South Africa.

In other ways, and not only from a statistical point of view, Underwood's fulfilment was adversely affected by administrative intervention — notably in the way the game and playing conditions were commercially tailored to fit the standard, medium-sized player and the undiscerning customer. Underwood was neither, just as he was neither a slow left-arm spinner nor a medium-pace seamer. He successfully marshalled all the bowling arts, save outright pace, and, when pitches were covered to eliminate the sticky dog — or even the damp pup — he attacked the batsman with a metronomic, mesmeric accuracy that defied, rather than invited, them to attack him. Underwood was never in the business of buying wickets.

It was part of what his critics regarded as dogma. He persisted in an over-long, flat-footed run up and a seemingly invariable attitude of delivery, too fast and too flat. But batsmen saw it — or, more pertinently, didn't see it — differently. Here was potentially dangerous subtlety skilfully disguised, for in Underwood's textbook traps were set to the half-inch and baited with a split second. And the combination could be critical. Deadly, in fact, which was the soubriquet bestowed on him by his peers and which was, in itself, an amiable antinomy.

It was true of Rocky Marciano, the awesome American heavyweight, that one could not find a kinder, more gentle spirit outside the ring nor a more

DEREK UNDERWOOD

Underwood in typical pose for Kent in 1978 — his England career was interrupted after his involvement with World Series cricket but his county career continued until 1987.

ruthless destroyer when summoned by the sound of bell and battle. So, too, albeit with rather more finesse, it was with Underwood. Off the field, a most genial and personable chap; at high noon on the square, a fierce competitor with the mind of a Tax Inspector. That said, the intensity of purpose was seldom more than frown-deep and the fall of a wicket would invariably release an eruption of glee that revealed the inner schoolboy innocent of all but the unashamed pleasure of personal and collective achievement. And there were days when Underwood's cup of joy was frequently replenished — even when the statutes were set against him and his kind.

At Canterbury in 1984, during the match against Hampshire, overnight rain proved too much for the obligatory covers and, when play began, an ominous dark patch lay on a length. Those who had played and watched cricket only in recent years had never seen Underwood bowl in such conditions. They were to witness an unforgettable — probably unrepeatable — phenomenon. Within 90 minutes so ruthlessly had he exploited the pitch that, in 11.2 overs, he claimed 7 wickets for 21 runs as Hampshire hurtled to defeat.

All of which evoked, among those with longer memories, the final Test at the Oval in 1968 when the 20-year-old Underwood produced a match-winning 7 for 50 to square the series against Bill Lawry's Australians. Here was the young artist in his element. Heavy morning rain had flooded the outfield and, after scores of volunteers had joined the ground-staff in mopping up, only 75 minutes of play was in prospect. Australia, with five wickets in hand, seemed certain to hold out for a draw.

So began an agonising race against time that ended when, with five minutes to spare, Underwood took his fourth wicket in 27 balls. A remarkable, if not untypical performance when such conditions prevailed, but an equally valid indication of Underwood's total skill is to be found in his bowling analysis for the first Australian innings in that same match — played on a perfect pitch which yielded 494 runs for England and 324 for Australia. In taking two wickets Underwood yielded only 1.7 runs for each of his 54 overs. Such economy — and stamina— seldom deserted him.

It has to be said that the texture of Underwood's bowling had infinitely greater subtlety and variety than that of his batting which, nevertheless, shared the common denominator of unstinting application. It consisted chiefly of four

DEREK UNDERWOOD

strokes: the forward defensive lunge, the backfoot defensive parry, the squat, forearm pull and the hunch-shouldered punch past point.

This limited repertoire served him well enough over the years, not least when he raised an unbeaten 48 off those same Australians of 1968. Even so, it was very much with feelings of wistful regret rather than surprise that Underwood reached his fortieth year before recording his first and only century. Almost inevitably it came at the Central Ground, Hastings — now regrettably passed from the first-class scene — where, in June 1964, Underwood had enjoyed another remarkable success in achieving a career-best bowling analysis of 9 for 28.

Needless to say, the cherished century was realised in the not unfamiliar role of night-watchman — a circumstance which had always offered the best hope on two counts. First, it afforded him the time to score runs but, more importantly, the initial situation was sufficiently grave to arouse Underwood's foremost, i.e. stubborn, instincts. Accordingly, lunge by lunge, swat by swat, he clawed his way to the nineties, at which point — and only at this point — did the prospect of a maiden century begin to intrude on the principal resolution to do his best for the side. In the event both considerations were gloriously accomplished and joy was unconfined — not only among his Kent colleagues but throughout the Sussex team and the entire assembly. That is the measure of the man's popularity and esteem.

D. L. UNDERWOOD KENT
BORN 8.6.45, BROMLEY, KENT

BATTING

	Matches	Innings	Not out	Runs	High score	Avg	100
Test	86	116	35	937	45*	11.56	0
First class	676	710	200	5,165	111	10.12	1

BOWLING AND FIELDING

	Runs	Wickets	Avg	5 W/I	10 W/M	BB	Ct	St
Test	7,674	297	25.83	17	6	8/51	44	0
First class	49,993	2,465	20.28	153	47	9/28	261	0

cricket heroes

HEDLEY VERITY

Tony Pawson

All Quiet on the Western Front ends on the note that amid the millions of victims of war just one death can be especially poignant. So it was when the news came that Captain Hedley Verity had been killed in July 1943 leading his company into attack in Sicily.

From a dominant Yorkshire team of great cricketers and characters he may well have been the greatest and best loved. Certainly he had already written his cricket epitaph in the grand manner in his final game. Yorkshire were playing at Hove when the message came through to finish the match quickly as war was imminent. Verity responded by taking 7 wickets for 9 runs in 6 overs as Sussex were hustled out for 33. That was nothing special for a man who once took 10 for 10 and averaged 173 wickets a season throughout his sadly abbreviated career.

It was fitting too that Verity had become a captain, even if an army one. For in the pre-war days when only amateurs were considered for captaincy, Douglas Jardine wrote that Verity was the ideal man to lead his country. That of course was another black mark from the establishment against Jardine, that very shrewd England captain whom they had pilloried and betrayed after he had won the bodyline series. This was the rest of Jardine's summary of the man whose slow left-arm bowling had made him second only to Larwood in the averages of those who took more than ten wickets in the 1932/33 Test series, noted for the fire and fury of the fast bowling:

"If Verity is compared with his three illustrious Yorkshire predecessors including Wilfred Rhodes I would need much convincing before awarding the palm to any of them in preference to him. In particular I venture to doubt if any bowler of his type has proved such a master on all kinds of wicket. So many slow left-handers only put on that extra 5 yards of pace when the wicket suits them, but Verity gives maximum effort all the time."

"Neither in Australia nor in England have I ever seen Verity thoroughly collared with all that that implies. He does not know what to give up trying means. He has, moreover, the unusual accomplishment of being able to change at will from over to round the wicket without any loss of accuracy. The oldest head on young shoulders in England cricket today is his. He can teach, nor is

Hedley Verity bowling for the championship-winning Yorkshire side against the Rest at the Oval in 1935.

HEDLEY VERITY

he above learning. It is a pleasure to see him set his field and having set it to bowl to it. No captain could have a greater asset on his side than Verity. He would make a great captain himself and will yet make a lot of runs with the bat."

Control and accuracy were a main feature of his bowling as was well illustrated in that 1932/33 series. On perfect Australian wickets against the likes of Bradman and McCabe, who might have been expected to turn on him with venom as a relief from facing Larwood, Voce and Allen, he bowled 117 maidens out of his 298.2 overs in those Tests. His 5 for 33 won the 5th Test and the only Test we lost rather than won was the second when an extra fast bowler (his Yorkshire colleague Bill Bowes) was played instead.

His value as a correct and studious batsman who had modelled himself on Herbert Sutcliffe was also apparent in this series as his two partnerships of 90 or more with Paynter were crucial to the winning of the third and fourth Tests. In a later series he also emulated Rhodes by opening an innings in a Test, going in first at Adelaide and scoring 17 and 19. But what made him quite outstanding as a cricketer was the spin and lift he could put on the ball as his height of almost 6 ft was enhanced by a high classical action. He was criticised by the old school, just as Underwood was to be later, for being too mechanical and pushing the ball through too fast without the cunning flight of a Rhodes. But like Underwood he had found a style which was even more effective and economical. Rhodes, not one to throw compliments around, accepted him as a near equal. But when asked if Verity could bowl any ball he couldn't he replied: "Yes. The one that is cut for four."

There were very few of these from Verity as this dedicated student of the game rapidly absorbed the teachings of his hard Yorkshire taskmasters, Rhodes and Hirst, who ruthlessly analysed every performance. There was no praise for him for taking 7 for 26, Rhodes's only comment being that it would have been 7 for 22 but for a boundary unnecessarily conceded.

Verity was born at Headingley on 18th May 1905, but with all the talent available in Yorkshire it was relatively late before his special gifts were recognised. He played for Yeadon secondary school, progressed to Yorkshire Council cricket for Rowdon, then to the Lancashire League as professional for Accrington and then Middleton. Aged 25 he had his first half season in the

HEDLEY VERITY

county team in 1930 taking 64 wickets at 12.48 apiece. His next season was sensational for someone with so little experience. His 188 wickets at 13.52 made him one of *Wisden's* players of the year and won him a place in two Tests against New Zealand in one of which he took 4 for 85. He also achieved in his first full season the feat which had eluded Rhodes despite playing first class cricket to the age of 52. For Verity took all 10 wickets for 36 against Warwickshire, one of many remarkable analyses which put him second in the national averages. Other striking performances were 6 for 21 and 8 for 33 against Glamorgan and 6 for 11 against Surrey. Inevitably Yorkshire won the championship, with Verity and Sutcliffe the key figures well supported by Bowes. Indeed, Bowes and Verity were to ensure such Yorkshire dominance of the thirties that only in 1934, weakened by Test calls, and 1936, did Yorkshire fail to take the title.

Verity in action for Yorkshire against Surrey at the Oval in 1937.

In all matches Verity was to take 1,956 wickets — 1,558 for Yorkshire at 13.71 apiece. In the Test cricket of the Bradman era, when many other bowlers were slaughtered, he took 144 wickets at an average of 24.37, and also 30 catches. As remarkable was his accuracy and low run rate per over. There were exceptions. The South African Herbie Cameron hit him for 30 in one over prompting wicketkeeper Wood's quote: "You had him in two minds Hedley. He didn't know whether to hit you for four or six." He was also hit for 28 in an over by an unexpected aggressor. Horace Hazell was no batsman and another member of the slow left-armers' union. Not quite as accurate as Verity, Horace was forever talking aloud urging himself to pitch the ball up, or give it more air. At the non-striker's end, listening to his chatter, I once asked: "Who is your friend, Horace?" The instant reply was: "Oh that's Harpic. Clean round the bend like me." Certainly he must have taken leave of his senses to hit Verity for four sixes and a four in one over.

Among Verity's many fine Test feats, the most memorable was that which won the second Test at Lord's to square the 1934 series. Australia were 192 for 2 overnight in reply to England's 440. But weekend rain affected the pitch and Verity became unplayable, taking 15 wickets as England won by an innings. As Jardine wrote at the time: "Verity's length was impeccable and he made the ball come back and lift so sharply that the Australians were helpless. Although the wicket certainly helped him it could not be described as 'sticky' except for

c r i c k e t   h e r o e s

HEDLEY VERITY

one period after lunch. This result was only possible for a man possessed of such finger-spin and accuracy as Verity."

The most remarkable of all his feats, however, was that nicely symmetrical analysis of 10 for 10 in just under 20 overs, 16 of them maidens. Appropriately it was on his home pitch of Headingley. A thunderstorm affected the wicket, but at lunch Nottinghamshire were 38 for 0. Soon they were 67 all out. In the course of that extraordinary destruction Verity did the hat trick and twice took two wickets in successive balls. To rub in the quality of his performance, Holmes and Sutcliffe scored the 139 runs to win in 90 minutes with no difficulty.

After that amazing first season in 1931 everyone wondered if Verity could sustain success. He did so year after year as he and Bill Bowes swapped places at the top of the bowling averages, or as he was the key to success for England's Test teams. The truest tribute came from a craftsman with words to a craftsman with the ball. The witty Robertson Glasgow, himself no mean bowler, thus summed up the virtues of the scholarly Verity:

"Some say Verity is not a great bowler. They are wrong. I have heard such adjectives as 'good' and 'mechanical' applied to him. The first is merely inadequate, the second is true in so far that he is nearly the perfect bowling machine directed by one of the most acute brains the game has known and kept in motion, against the best batsmen, by an indomitable courage."

"His prevailing pace is slow-medium though sometimes he likes to whisk down a yorker or inswinger which is nearly fast. Only on wet or dusty wickets does he bowl at a genuinely slow pace — and then not all the time. He is a scholarly bowler, graduating to judge by his enquiring attitudes in science and experimental philosophy rather than any romantic faculty. He is tall and much stronger than his pace needs. His run-up, longer than in most of his kind, has a measured delicacy that you expect from this fastidious and neatly prim craftsman. Only his delivery has a grace which mathematics can't explain. I have seen him in certain company become rather bored with his bowling and their batting, which is something of a weakness. A fellow Yorkshire bowler says that to get the best out of Verity you have to tell him that all depends on him which argues the vanity of the artist. As a batsman he looks like Sutcliffe gone stale. That is, pretty good..."

HEDLEY VERITY

To him as a person the final tribute comes from Douglas Jardine: "There will be few if any to dispute Verity's claim to be head and shoulders above the rest between the wars. No captain could have asked for a sounder counsellor or companion on and off the field or one better endowed with that sturdy equable humour untouched by failure or success. He will be missed by those who really knew him, as a man."

H. VERITY YORKSHIRE
BORN 18.5.05, HEADINGLEY, LEEDS, YORKSHIRE

BATTING

	Matches	Innings	Not out	Runs	High score	Avg	100
Test	40	44	12	669	66*	20.90	0
First class	378	416	106	5,605	101	18.08	1

BOWLING AND FIELDING

	Runs	Wickets	Avg	5 W/I	10 W/M	BB	Ct	St
Test	3,510	144	24.37	5	2	8/43	30	0
First class	29,146	1,956	14.90	164	54	10/10	269	0

cricket heroes

ARTHUR WELLARD

David Foot

Arthur Wellard was a cherished but expensive adornment to the first-class game. He lost more balls than any other cricketer. While many of his contemporaries took inordinate delight, as batsmen, in describing an artistic arc with glides and deflections, controlled pulls and carpeted drives, Arthur braced those broad Kentish shoulders and aimed for distant allotments, railway sidings (once into a passing goods wagon from where the ball was never retrieved), the River Tone and vulnerable passing traffic on adjacent roads. He did it with a deadpan expression, even though it was often a comic process. His respect for the bowler would usually be manifested with an exaggerated straight bat for the first over or so. Then, with no more than a token backlift, he proceeded to endanger circling gulls at Hove or starlings reckless enough to perch in the loftier conifers around long-on area at Weston.

He especially liked Wells, more for its short boundaries we must assume than its ecclesiastical decorum. Derbyshire's Tom Armstrong was belted for five sixes in an over and, two years later, Kent's Frank Woolley suffered a similar indignity. The crowd seemed half composed of theological students, who wisely kept one eye on the heavens as the ball kept dropping disconcertingly to earth amid a flutter of cassocks. Woolley had had enough after two overs (0-40) and retired to the outfield. Wellard also dismissed him twice leg-before in that same match; for a man of less generous nature, it would have almost looked like a vendetta.

Because cricket is such a romantic and quirky game, we tend to remember Arthur Wellard primarily for his batting, unorthodox though it was. Aged Somerset spectators still tell you they saw most of his 72 sixes in 1935 — a national record superseded by Ian Botham exactly half a century later — and momentarily, reprehensibly, forget his bowling. He was fast-medium, with a high action and a hint of a leap as he reached the wicket. The ball swung away from the right-hander or might break back wickedly. He took 1,614 wickets, a hundred wickets in a season eight times, and in 1929 did the hat-trick against Leicestershire. Arthur at one end and his devoted friend, Bill Andrews, the inswinger, soon to be at the other — a formidable and ever-convivial new ball attack in the years running up to the war.

c r i c k e t   h e r o e s

ARTHUR WELLARD

Wellard was an all-rounder in the most comprehensive sense. Three times he did the double. And his big hands, either at slip or at silly mid-off, never failed him. He held on to 375 catches, often demonstrating an intrepid nature and, for a big easy-going man, the sharpest of reflexes. When fielding in front of the wicket on a hot afternoon, he was known to take out his false teeth and put them in his pocket. It changed his appearance markedly and the cunning old campaigner knew it. "I don't mind you standing there breathing down my shirt front, but for heaven's sake, put your bloody dentures back in," one Glamorgan skipper pleaded.

No-one is too sure how Kent let him slip away. He arrived in the West Country with what seemed like a cockney accent and the flashiest suit any of the players at Taunton had ever seen. Half the team began to hero-worship him, not only the pros. Out of season he played football; in the dressing room he played solo or poker with far too much skill for the other cricketers sheltering from the rain. He was a friendly, dry-humoured man, never garrulous. He liked a bet and would pass on a tip. If there was an evening race meeting at Bath during the festival, he'd be the first man dressed and away. After play at Bristol, he would follow the dogs at Eastville. A friend claimed Wellard had special pockets built into the fronts of his trousers. That was where he kept his notes at the races; he argued that pickpockets could too easily get at his money in a back pocket.

Wellard, a big, commanding figure with plenty of basic wisdom, was something of an elder statesman in the dressing room. He delegated Andrews to go to the secretary in search of better terms. Arthur went himself in 1948 when Gimblett had scored his 310 at Eastbourne. Brigadier Lancaster, once of the Indian Army, was then the secretary. He was a tall, erect, rather distant figure, somewhat too military in bearing for most of the professionals. "Brigadier," said Wellard, never too overawed by rank, "we've got to recognise Harold's knock, somehow or other. I think we ought to have a collection round the ground for our next home match." The idea was rejected and Wellard banged the door as he went out of the office.

Wellard would cuss at what he saw as injustice. He was wary of cricket officials with too much power and loquacious committee members who didn't really understand the game. Some of the other players could articulate the

c r i c k e t   h e r o e s

ARTHUR WELLARD

day's nuances better. He was an uncomplicated man who ran his thick, eloquent fingers along the seam and got on with it. By way of variation, he would adeptly turn to off spinners.

At Somerset he was the most spectacular all-rounder they had had since Sammy Woods. He dressed better than Sammy, whether it was revealed by the crease in his flannels or the polish on his shoes. He had a pride in the craft of cricket — and his pride was hurt when the county told him, with relative tact by their own standards, that it was time to go. "He walked around with his bootlaces undone, something we'd never seen before," a team-mate told me.

Arthur went into the league, where his exciting, personalised technique was immediately embraced. When into his seventies, he was offering kindly rebuke and ignoring rheumatism as he played for and umpired Harold Pinter's Gaieties. I was privileged to share the field with him in his final match, as part of Somerset's centenary celebrations at Weston's Clarence Park in 1975. He opened the bowling, the arm no longer quite at 12 o'clock, with Bill — there were moist eyes and laughter.

There was one Test against New Zealand in 1937 and one against the Aussies the following year. He would have gone to India on the 1939-40 tour but for the war. "Yet I'd already been there, old cock," he would say with mock worldliness. "Went on tour with Lord Tennyson. Hure... [the welcome West Country inflection] Did I ever tell you about that tiger shoot?" It was his favourite story. But for those who went to watch him at Taunton, Bath, Weston and Wells, every innings of Wellard's was a story worth telling.

A. W. WELLARD SOMERSET
BORN 8.4.02, SOUTHFLEET, KENT

BATTING

	Matches	Innings	Not out	Runs	High score	Avg	100
Test	2	4	0	47	38	11.75	0
First class	417	679	46	12,485	112	19.72	2

BOWLING AND FIELDING

	Runs	Wickets	Avg	5 W/I	10 W/M	BB	Ct	St
Test	237	7	33.85	0	0	4/81	2	0
First class	39,302	1,614	24.35	108	24	8/52	375	0

cricket heroes

BOB WILLIS

Alan Lee

Since the heady days of John Snow's pomp, England has produced only one great fast bowler in virtually 20 years and to say that he was a misfit who conquered long odds is to do the case little justice. Bob Willis resembled the photofit image of the top quick bowler in neither body nor brain, yet through an intense desire to succeed he became, for a time, the most prolific English wicket-taker in the history of Test cricket. When Willis retired, at the end of the 1984 season, he had taken 325 wickets in 90 Tests. This despite serious injuries brought about by a gangling physique ill-suited to the punishing, pounding routine and, in addition, a complex, fretful personality not altogether ideal for his essentially simple role.

It must be one of the heaviest regrets of those running the England team that, for so much of his career, Willis did not have a regular partner with the new ball. It may be a cliche to say that fast bowlers hunt best in pairs but it is also undoubtedly true; the history of the game is littered with the evidence. If Willis's time had coincided with Snow's, who can say how much richer England's fortunes might have been? Sadly, after four successful liaisons on the triumphant Ashes tour of 1970-71, they didn't play together again until the fourth Test of 1976, the last of Snow's turbulent career. Injuries were partly to blame but so too were other, less persuasive factors. It amounted to a shocking waste of potentially rewarding resources. For the remainder of his career, Willis had a bewildering variety of partners. At the tail-end of the 1970s, Ian Botham's ability to swing the new ball created an effectively contrasting strike team; then, early in the 1980s, it seemed that Graham Dilley would become the hostile ally he had long sought. But Botham's bowling flagged along with Dilley's fitness and Willis ploughed a lonely furrow once more.

Not that one would have said he suffered from solitude; in other respects, he positively sought it. Willis was at his quirkiest on the eve of a big match. His nerves were legendary and they became no less of a problem for the familiarity of such occasions. He was almost ten years an England player when he began to resort to hypnotherapy to calm him and channel his motivation away from negative thoughts. He swore by the process and was influential in introducing it to other, similarly afflicted sportsmen.

Another victim for Bob Willis as Mohsin Khan of Pakistan is caught behind the wicket.

c r i c k e t   h e r o e s

BOB WILLIS

At times of stress Willis was poor company — distracted, introverted and thoroughly gloomy. He is, however, a man of contradictions and when the pressure was off, at the end of a game or, ideally, away from cricket altogether, he was invariably the life and soul of any party, his manic sense of humour utterly infectious.

He is and always has been a lover of music, though his tastes have changed from the obsessional following for Bob Dylan which accounts for his self-added third forename, to a liking of classics and the opera. It was the rhythms and laments of Dylan which accompanied him throughout his early, tearaway years in the game and which sit comfortably with his personality. To call Willis a rebel might be to slight a man of certain reactionary views, but his opinions have always been strongly formulated and firmly aired.

It was thought that he would stay active in the game and, indeed, he set out to do so in a managerial role, first with the Young England side and then the full touring team to the Caribbean in 1986. That disastrous tour demanded scapegoats, however, and Willis suffered more than any.

Just conceivably, he is happier without any direct involvement in cricket. The game certainly gave him more than his share of heartaches. In 1975, when he ought to have been approaching his peak, his knees gave out under the unnatural strain of supporting his 6 foot 6 inch frame thumping into the return crease dozens of time a day. The knees were operated upon simultaneously in April of that year and pessimists pondered his chances of ever bowling fast again. Yet he was back in action before the end of the summer and returned to the England side against the 1976 West Indians. There, occasional injury and illness aside, he was to stay until his 90th and final Test eight years later.

Along the way, he dallied with the two great temptations of the era and narrowly resisted them both. In 1977 he closely considered an offer to join Kerry Packer's World Series Cricket before ultimately rejecting it and becoming vociferous against the project. Then, in 1982, he was offered the captaincy of the unofficial English party to tour South Africa. He gave it serious thought but, as he later recalled: "I turned it down for the same reasons that I turned down World Series Cricket. I had become establishment-minded and could still not imagine being sufficiently motivated by international matches which were not what they claimed to be." With supreme irony, he was made captain of

Crowe of New Zealand is comprehensively beaten to give Willis his 300th Test wicket.

BOB WILLIS

England two months later. It was a job he had seldom contemplated, much less coveted, despite being vice-captain on various overseas tours. He had been at home in that job, using his undoubted powers of motivation off the field and concentrating on his bowling once the game began. Perhaps he was not so effective in total charge, though he did lead England to victory in three consecutive home series, a record which would be welcomed now.

He played his final game for England at the age of 35, advanced for a fast bowler, and he was already 31 when he guaranteed his place in cricket folklore with that astonishing, match-winning spell at Headingley in 1981. Botham's century had turned the game but Willis's inspired bowling, delivered by a man who might easily have been in a trance, secured the most famous win in recent England history. If anyone has ever bowled with more obsessional intensity for England I should like to have seen it. The image of that day is how Willis will always be remembered.

Bob Willis: obssessional intensity.

R. G. D. WILLIS SURREY AND WARWICKSHIRE
BORN 30.5.49, SUNDERLAND, COUNTY DURHAM

BATTING

	Matches	Innings	Not out	Runs	High score	Avg	100
Test	90	128	55	840	28*	11.50	0
First class	308	333	145	2,690	72	14.30	0

BOWLING AND FIELDING

	Runs	Wickets	Avg	5 W/I	10 W/M	BB	Ct	St
Test	8,190	325	25.20	16	0	8/43	39	0
First class	22,468	899	24.99	34	2	8/32	134	0

cricket heroes

FRANK WOOLLEY

E. W. Swanton

Frank Woolley was a cricketer of the Golden Age, and in particular of Kent's golden age. His arrival in 1906 and swift maturing coincided with the county's first era of supremacy wherein within eight years they won four Championships. They did so with what seems in retrospect an ideal and enviable blend of amateur and professional — and it was this combination which gives us the key to Frank's cricket. When he first blossomed as a tall, slim 19-year-old, J. T. Tyldesley was the only professional who could hold an undoubted place in the England XI as a batsman. In Kent's first Championship year the first five places in the batting averages were filled by amateurs. Brought up in the Kent nursery at Tonbridge, his birth-place, Woolley saw their glamorous style of play as a lad, and determined that in order to succeed their methods should be his.

Frank Woolley's arrival at Kent coincided with the county's run of four Championships within eight seasons.

He wasted little time. The first of his 145 hundreds, made against Hampshire a few days after his debut, fittingly at Tonbridge, took him an hour and a half. He had gone in with the score at 23 for three. From the start his batting embodied the spirit of Kent cricket as it then was; very soon he was excelling all in the attractiveness of his play, just as Jack Hobbs had begun to do for Surrey at the Oval a year earlier. How lucky it was for the game that these two superb cricketers emerged when they did, as examples to their profession — off the field, be it said, as well as on.

Frank, of course, had two strings to his bow — indeed three since his tally of 1,018 catches (mostly at slip) has never been approached. Though it is his batting which has ensured his enduring fame, he and Colin Blythe made a formidable combination of slow left-arm bowling for Kent. Both were considerable spinners of the ball, Blythe also a master of flight, his younger partner with a steep trajectory which made him specially difficult on wet pitches. He once took 10 for 54 against Australia at the Oval. Until 1923 he regularly took over 100 wickets a season and only 26 men in history have exceeded his career total of 2,068. His mountain of runs, 58,969, has been bettered only by Hobbs. Four times he scored 2,000 runs and took 100 wickets in a season. No-one else has achieved that, though George Hirst's 2,385 runs and 208 wickets stands as the unachievable peak of all-roundedness.

c r i c k e t   h e r o e s